D1462674

Ancient Philosophy: A Very Short Introduction

'This book, written by one of the best-known scholars in the subject, offers a fresh and original approach to introducing readers to ancient philosophy. . . . Annas explores six themes as a way of alerting modern readers to the interest and challenge of ancient philosophy. . . . the writing is lively and non-technical, [and] Annas opens up a range of very important questions about ancient thought and about modern reception of antiquity.'
Christopher Gill, University of Exeter

'A+ for Annas on Ancient Philosophy. This should be the first book any prospective student in philosophy reads. Annas's renowned scholarship, combined with her engaging style, enable her to convey an astonishing amount about the ancient Greeks and still find room for many fascinating insights into how their thought relates to the way we think now and how it was interpreted in earlier centuries.'
Rosalind Hursthouse, The Open University

VERY SHORT INTRODUCTIONS are for anyone wanting a stimulating and accessible way in to a new subject. They are written by experts, and have been published in more than 25 languages worldwide.

The series began in 1995, and now represents a wide variety of topics in history, philosophy, religion, science, and the humanities. Over the next few years it will grow to a library of around 200 volumes – a Very Short Introduction to everything from ancient Egypt and Indian philosophy to conceptual art and cosmology.

Very Short Introductions available now:

Available soon:

For more information visit our web site
www.oup.co.uk/vsi

Julia Annas

ANCIENT PHILOSOPHY

A Very Short Introduction

OXFORD
UNIVERSITY PRESS

OXFORD
UNIVERSITY PRESS

Great Clarendon Street, Oxford OX2 6DP

Oxford University Press is a department of the University of Oxford.
It furthers the University's objective of excellence in research, scholarship,
and education by publishing worldwide in

Oxford New York

Auckland Bangkok Buenos Aires Cape Town Chennai
Dar es Salaam Delhi Hong Kong Istanbul Karachi Kolkata
Kuala Lumpur Madrid Melbourne Mexico City Mumbai Nairobi
São Paulo Shanghai Taipei Tokyo Toronto

Oxford is a registered trade mark of Oxford University Press
in the UK and in certain other countries

Published in the United States
by Oxford University Press Inc., New York

British Library Cataloguing in Publication Data
Data available

Library of Congress Cataloging in Publication Data
Data available

ISBN 978-0-19-285357-8

9 10

Typeset by RefineCatch Ltd, Bungay, Suffolk
Printed in Great Britain by
Ashford Colour Press Ltd, Gosport, Hampshire

Preface

The prospect of writing a *very* short introduction to ancient philosophy has attracted and intrigued me for some time. I would like to thank Shelley Cox for her encouragement and comments, as well as Christopher Gill, Laura Owen, David Owen, and a reader for Oxford University Press. I would like to thank Cindy Holder for help with the proofs and index. Needless to say, the shortcomings rest with me. I would like to dedicate this book to the memory of my friend Jean Hampton, who I hope would have enjoyed it.

Contents

List of Illustrations

Introduction

A very short introduction should have modest aims. It is also, however, an opportunity to give the reader direct ways into the subject, and lead him or her straight off to what is most important about the subject. In this book I have tried to engage the reader with ancient philosophy in the way that matters, as a tradition of discussion and engagement, a conversation which I hope will continue after the reader has finished this book.

Because I have focused on important and revealing features of ancient philosophy, I have not tried to work through a standard chronological account of the tradition. Not only does the *very* short nature of this book make that a bad idea (since the tradition is too rich to cram into a very short account), but there is no shortage of books available that will help the beginner deepen his or her interest in ancient philosophy. The list of Further Reading indicates good places to start; beginners have never been better served with reference books, translations and companions than they are today.

I start by introducing the reader, in Chapter 1 ('Humans and beasts: understanding ourselves') to an issue in ancient philosophy, about understanding the conflict of reason and emotion within ourselves, an issue which is readily understandable and one that a modern reader can engage with before knowing much about the background of the theories involved. I am hoping to get across the centrality to the ancient tradition of argument, and also of practical engagement with issues important to our lives. In the second chapter ('Why do we read Plato's *Republic*?') I focus, by contrast, on factors that distance us from the ancient philosophical writers. One is the literal distance of time and the loss of much evidence. Another is the influence of other factors, which we should be aware of, which make our concern with the ancients a selective and changeable one, so that a text like Plato's *Republic* is read very differently at different times. Both the immediacy and the distance are things we should be aware of. In Chapters 3 and 4 ('The happy life, ancient and modern' and 'Reason, knowledge and scepticism') I show how we can understand and engage with the ancient variety of views on ethics and on knowledge – how we can come to engage with the ancients in a respectful but critical way, both disagreeing with them and learning from them. Chapter 5 ('Logic and reality') takes up the rest of the ancient philosophy syllabus, focusing on one particular metaphysical debate, namely whether there are purposes in nature or not, and if so what they are. Chapter 6 ('When did it all begin? (and what is it anyway?)') raises the issue of what, if anything, unites the ancient philosophical tradition. This is a question better asked at the end than at the beginning of an account of it, since I hope that the reader will agree that the main lines of what I say have emerged from the previous chapters. (And if she disagrees, this will, I hope, be in the spirit of the debates which have been covered.)

However, if you are quite new to the subject you might appreciate a quick chronological sketch of the tradition you are being so briefly introduced to, so one follows. There is also a timeline placing the major figures in ancient philosophy, not all of whom can be adequately dealt with in this book, though many are discussed in the text and the text-boxes.

Ancient philosophy is traditionally held to begin in the sixth century BC, in the Greek cities of coastal Asia Minor. A large number of philosophers are generally grouped as 'Presocratics'; their activities cover the sixth and fifth centuries. Thales, Anaximander and Anaximenes are early cosmologists, giving ambitious accounts of the world as a whole. Pythagoras began a tradition emphasizing mysticism and authority. Heraclitus produced notoriously obscure aphorisms. Xenophanes begins a long concern with knowledge and its grounds.

Parmenides and Zeno became famous for arguments which apparently cannot be refuted but which reach conclusions impossible to accept. These arguments provoke a crisis in philosophical accounts of the world; responses to it can be found in the cosmologies of Anaxagoras, Empedocles and the Atomists Leucippus and Democritus.

In the second half of the fifth century, intellectuals called sophists developed some philosophical skills, particularly in argument, and philosophical interests, particularly in ethical and social thought. The best known are Protagoras, Hippias, Gorgias and Prodicus.

Some of these people are not strictly *Pre*socratics, since their lives overlapped with that of Socrates, but Socrates is generally held to mark a turning-point in ancient philosophy. He wrote nothing, but greatly influenced a number of followers, including Aristippus, a founder of hedonism, the idea that our aim should be pleasure, and Antisthenes, a founder of Cynicism, the idea that our needs should be as minimal as possible. Socrates' emphasis on questioning and argument made him the key symbolic figure of the Philosopher to the ancient world.

Socrates' most famous follower is Plato, the best-known ancient philosopher, who wrote a number of philosophical dialogues famous for their literary skill. Plato founded the first philosophical school, and he and his most famous pupil, Aristotle, dominate the philosophy of the fourth century. Both left extensive works – Plato in finished form, Aristotle in the form of lecture and research notes.

The 'Hellenistic' period (traditionally from 323 BC, the death of Alexander the Great, to the end of the Roman republic at the end of the first century BC) was marked by the emergence of two new philosophical schools, those of Epicurus and the Stoics, and also of philosophical movements which were not institutionalized as schools, such as the Cynics, and Pyrrho, the first sceptic. Plato's school practised a form of scepticism in this period, and several mixed or hybrid schools tried to bring together the insights of different schools of thought.

During the first century BC to the second century AD, the early Roman empire, the existing schools continue, and philosophy flourishes. No new major schools emerge, but there is renewed interest in Pythagoras, and also in studying Plato's ideas positively and systematically.

Late antiquity sees the emergence, in the second to third centuries, of an original new school, that of Plotinus, which revives some of Plato's ideas and is called 'Neoplatonism'. As Christianity becomes the official religion of the Roman empire, which divides into an eastern and a western part, the dominant world-view becomes Platonism, and this is the tradition most influential on Christianity. The first major western Christian thinker, Augustine, is influenced by Platonism, but has already lost touch with the major traditions of ancient philosophical thinking.

Chapter 1

Humans and beasts: understanding ourselves

Medea's revenge

Medea, daughter of the King of Colchis, has betrayed her country and family out of love for the Greek adventurer Jason, who has brought her back to Greece. Now they have fallen on hard times, and to mend his fortunes Jason has left Medea and their two sons and is to marry the daughter of the King of Corinth. He does not understand the depth of her outrage; her sacrifice and devotion mean little to him. Medea realizes that there is only one way to bring home to Jason what he has done, what kind of commitment he has discounted. The only way to hurt him as much as he has hurt her is to kill their sons, depriving him of any descendants and leaving his life empty. But can she do this? They are her children too.

In Euripides' famous play, produced at Athens in the fifth century BC, Medea resolves to kill her sons, then goes back on her resolve when she sees them. Sending them away, she steels herself to do the deed, and speaks words which were to become famous:

> I know that what I am about to do is bad, but anger is master of my plans,
> which is the source of the greatest troubles for humankind.

She recognizes two things going on in her: her plans and her anger or *thumos*. She also recognizes that her anger is 'master of' the plans she has rationally deliberated on carrying out.

What is going on here? We may think that nothing is going on that a philosopher needs to concern herself with; we simply have something which happens every day, though usually not in such spectacular ways. I think it better for me to do A than B, but am led by anger, or some other emotion, to do B instead.

But how do we understand what is going on? How can I genuinely think that A is the better thing to do, if I end up doing B? How can anger, or any other emotion or feeling, get someone to go against what they have deliberately resolved on doing? Until we have some systematic way of understanding this, we and the way we act are mysterious to ourselves. Many people, of course, do remain this way, with many of the sources of their actions and their patterns of behaviour opaque to themselves. But the society in which Euripides' play was produced and continued to be a classic fostered a kind of thinking, the kind we call philosophical thinking. This kind of reflective, probing thinking regarded Medea's situation as calling for explanation and understanding in terms that they, and we so many years later, can readily recognize as philosophical.

As already indicated, the question of what, if anything, distinguishes ancient philosophy and its methods will emerge by the end of the book; here we will focus on an issue where we can readily understand what ancient philosophers are doing.

The Stoics: the soul as a unity

Are there really two distinct things operating in Medea, her plans and her furious anger? How do they relate to Medea herself, who is so lucidly aware of what is going on? One school of ancient philosophers, the Stoics, developed a distinctive view of Medea as part of their ethics and

Stoicism is a philosophical school named after the Stoa Poikile or Painted Porch, a colonnaded building in Athens where the first heads of the school taught. The school was founded by Zeno of Citium, who arrived in Athens in 313 BC. After Zeno the most influential head of the school was Chrysippus of Soli (c.280–208 BC) who wrote extensively on just about every philosophical topic, and produced what became authoritative Stoic positions.

Stoicism often presented itself, particularly at first, in a deliberately harsh light, emphasizing doctrines that are so far from common sense as to be paradoxical. However, Stoicism as a philosophy is holistic – that is, its parts can be developed separately, but ultimately the aim is to understand them all in relation to the other parts. Hence Stoic 'paradoxes' increasingly make sense and acquire conviction as they are appreciated against the background of Stoic arguments and connected ideas. There are thus many ways of teaching Stoicism; where you begin depends on the audience's level of interest and expertise. Epictetus, a later Stoic (AD c.50–130), taught in a way that appealed directly to his audience's interest in ethical and social matters, and accounts of his teaching have continued to be used as a vivid introduction to Stoic thought. The universal aspect of Stoicism is illustrated by the fact that Epictetus, a former slave, was influential on the Stoic reflections of the emperor Marcus Aurelius (AD 121–180).

psychology. They think that the idea that there are really two distinct forces or motives at work in Medea is an illusion. What matters in this situation is always *Medea* herself, the person, and it is wrong to think in terms of different parts of her. After all, she is quite clear about how her thoughts are going. First she resolves to do one thing, then to do another – but these are both *her* resolves, decisions that she comes to as a result of giving weight to resentment on the one hand or love on the other.

Medea as a whole veers now in one direction, now in another. How then can she come to a considered judgement as to what to do, and then act on anger which is stronger than this? What happens, the Stoics think, is that, being in an emotional state, she follows the reasons which go with that state: she seeks revenge because that is how angry people think. But there is no real division within Medea's self. She oscillates between different decisions as a whole; there is no inner battle of parts of her. She is like the example Chrysippus used to explain emotion: a runner who is going too fast to stop, and so is out of control *as a whole*. When, therefore, she says that anger is master of her plans, what is meant is that anger is in control of them; she is reasoning, but the way she does it has been taken over by anger and achieves its aims. The angry person does not cease to reason – he doesn't act blindly – but his reasoning is in the service of anger.

The Stoics think that there are no parts or divisions to the human soul, and that it is all rational. (By the soul they mean the item that makes humans live in a characteristically human way.) Emotions are not blind, non-rational forces which can overcome rational resolve; they are themselves a kind of reason which the person determines to act on. 'It is precisely this, gratifying her anger and being revenged on her husband, that she thinks more advantageous than saving her children,' says Epictetus, a later Stoic. Blind fury could not lead to Medea's carefully planned and self-aware revenge.

But, we say, Medea could not help acting as she did; she was overcome by passion, so surely she had no real choice. No, says Epictetus; she thought she had no real alternative, but this was wrong. She could have adjusted to her loss, difficult though this would be. 'Stop wanting your husband, and nothing you want will fail to come about,' he says.

Everything I do, I am responsible for; there is always something else I could have done, some other attitude I could have taken up. To say I am overcome by emotion is to evade the fact that I was the one who acted, who thought at the time that what I was doing was the right thing to do. Epictetus thinks that we should sympathize with Medea, who acted, after all, 'from a great spirit'; we can understand her reasons for revenge even when we see why she would have done better to reject

Plato of Athens (427–347 BC) is the best-known ancient philosopher, largely because he was also a great writer, and produced not philosophical treatises but a number of formally self-contained dialogues, many of which are attractive reading even for non-philosophers. Writing this way is not just for literary effect; the dialogue form formally distances Plato from the views of anyone in the dialogue, and this forces the reader to think for herself what positions are being discussed, and what the upshot is, rather than accepting what is said on Plato's authority.

Plato's ideas are original, bold and wide-ranging. But in the ancient world he was influential for the form of his philosophical activity as much as for the content. There were two major Platonic traditions. Firstly, the sceptical Academy, Plato's own school, for hundreds of years – until it came to an end in the first century BC – took its task to be that of arguing against the views of others without relying on a position of one's own. Secondly, the later Platonists, beginning from the first century BC, were interested in studying Plato's own ideas in a systematic way, and in teaching and furthering them. The relationship of the later, more positive tradition to the earlier, more negative one was varied and often contested.

Humans and beasts

them. 'She did not know where the power lies to do what we want – that this is not to be got from outside ourselves nor by changing and rearranging things.'

The Stoic view of emotions as a kind of reason is probably unfamiliar, and tends to sound odd when first introduced. I have also plunged into the middle of things by starting with the Stoics, who belong to the period of philosophy after Aristotle, often called 'Hellenistic'. We are likely to be more familiar with the philosophical interpretation of Medea that I shall now turn to. It appears nearer to common sense and it comes from Plato, an earlier and much better-known philosopher.

Plato: the soul has parts

Plato takes the phenomenon of psychological conflict, being torn between two options, to show that the person so torn is not really a unity; he is genuinely torn between the motivational pull of two or more distinct parts of the soul. Plato uses two examples. One is a person who strongly desires to drink, but reasons that he should not do so, probably because this would be bad for his health. He is, then, pulled towards taking the drink, and also, at the same time and in the same respect, pulled away from it. However, the argument goes, the same thing can't be thus affected in opposing ways at the same time, so it must be that it is not the person as a whole who is in this contradictory state, but different parts of him which do the pulling in opposite directions. When I reflect correctly, then, I can see that *I* don't want to drink and want not to drink; rather, part of me, which Plato calls desire, wants to drink, and another part of me, which is reason (my ability to grasp and act on reasons), is motivated to refrain.

Plato thinks that our psychological life is too complex to be accounted for purely in terms of reason and desire. There is a third part, called spirit or anger, and involving most of what we would call the emotions. It can conflict with desire, as Plato argues (in the fourth book of his work the *Republic*) from another case of conflict, where giving in to a pathological desire leads the person to feel angry and ashamed with himself. This emotional part is distinguished from reason, on the grounds that it is found in animals and children that don't reason; although it often endorses reason, it is essentially inarticulate and unable fully to grasp or to originate reasons.

The parts of the soul are not on a par; reason is not just a part but grasps the best interests of all the parts and hence of the person as a whole. Plato tirelessly insists that in the soul reason should rule, since it can understand its own needs and also those of the other parts, whereas the other parts are limited and short-sighted, alive only to their own needs and interests. The real contrast, then, is between reason, articulate guardian of the interests of the whole person, and the other parts, which can't look beyond their own needs. Hence it is not very surprising that, despite Plato's long imaginative descriptions of his three-part soul, the point of the idea was seen as that of contrasting a rational with a non-rational part of me, and so as compatible with a two-part soul.

If Plato is right, then when Medea resolves that it is best to spare her children, but is then led by fury to kill them, there is a real internal division and battle going on in her. Her reason works out what is for the best, but is then overwhelmed by another part of her soul, the furious anger, which is a separate source of motivation and in this case gets her to take what her reason sees to be the worse course.

Clearly Plato will take Medea's crucial lines to be saying that her reason works out what the best course is, but that anger thereupon turns out to be a stronger force, which overwhelms reason. And this might seem to be common sense; we do often have experiences that we are tempted to describe as inner conflict, with reason or passion winning because it is stronger. It seems more common-sensical at first than the Stoic claim that anger and other emotions *are* certain kinds of reason. And yet the Stoics do better than Plato in explaining how the person carried away by fury still can act in a self-aware, complex and planned way. Medea kills her children; horrible though this is, it is a deliberate action. She doesn't run amok. Can the anger that drives her really motivate her in a way that has nothing to do with reason?

There are two distinct ways that Plato's ideas can be developed when we think about inner conflict and the problems we have in understanding what is happening in us. Both of them are found in Plato, who clearly has not seen that he has to choose between them.

What is a 'part' of the soul, like anger or other emotions? So far, we have gone with a fairly intuitive idea; there seem to be two distinct sources of motivation within us. And we can form a fairly clear notion of the nature and function of the part which is reason. After all, we reason all the time, about the way things are or ought to be, and about what to do; and what in each case I am reasoning about is what *I* shall do, not what part of me shall do.

But what about the part of the soul that motivates me separately from reason? Can it be thought of as a purely irrational force? Although the language of passion fighting with and overwhelming reason might suggest this, it is hard to see how deliberate actions can be produced by something that is a completely irrational push. Surely there must be *something* in Medea's anger which is at least responsive to reason?

In many parts of his work Plato assumes that the parts of the soul are all sufficiently rational for them to communicate with and understand one another. They can all agree, in which case the person functions as an integrated whole. While the parts other than reason cannot do what reason can, namely think in terms of the person as a whole, they can still respond to what reason requires, and so understand it in a limited way. Desire, for example, can come to understand that reason forbids its satisfaction in certain circumstances, and so can come to adjust, not putting up a fight. Desire has thus been persuaded and educated by reason, rather than repressed. In terms of the whole person, when I see that some kind of action is wrong, I feel less desire to do it, and find it less difficult to refrain. Plato represents this position as one in which the soul's parts agree and are in harmony and concord. The parts other than reason have sufficient grip on what reason holds to be right that they willingly conform themselves to this, and the result is a harmonious and integrated personality.

This picture implies, though, that reason has a kind of internal hold on the other parts – it asks them, so to speak, to do things in terms that they can understand and agree to. But then won't the parts other than reason have to have a kind of reason of their own, in order to understand and go along with what the reason part demands? And then won't all the parts have to have their own reasons? – which makes it unclear how we are supposed to have found a part of the soul which is *separate* from reason.

Suppose there were some aspect of me which were entirely non-rational and separate from reason: this would indeed look like a different part of me, but with no reason internal to it at all, it is not clear how it can listen to reason, or conform itself to what reason requires in the interests of the whole person. Such a part looks like something sub-human. And indeed we find that in some of Plato's most famous passages about the divided soul he represents the parts of the soul other than reason as non-human animals. In one passage near the end of the *Republic* he says that we all contain a little human trying to control two animals. One part, spirit, is fierce, but stable and manageable – a lion. The other part, desire, is an unpredictable monster, constantly changing shape. Clearly Plato thinks that our emotions and desires are forces within us which are in themselves subhuman, but can be trained and moulded by reason to form part of a human life – indeed, of what he thinks to be the happiest form of human life.

Another passage, in the *Phaedrus*, is even more famous. The human soul is here a chariot, with reason, the charioteer, driving two horses. One horse is biddable and can learn to obey commands, but the other is both deaf and violent, and so can be controlled only by force. In a vivid passage Plato depicts the charioteer struggling to manage sexual desire, represented by the bad horse, only with great effort; that horse threatens to get out of control and has to be yanked back, struggling all the way. It learns to refrain only through fear of punishment.

There is something plausible in this picture as a picture of ourselves; it often does seem that we are motivated by forces within us that are resistant to the reasons that we accept. But if we think systematically of some of the consequences, the picture is considerably more disturbing. If part of me is properly to be represented as an animal, then there is part of me that is essentially less than human, and so not properly part of *me*. It becomes part of me only when subject to control by what really is me – reason. There is a kind of self-alienation at work here; part of me is regarded as being outside the self proper, because it is the kind of thing it is, and as being always potentially disobedient to my real self.

It is hard not to feel that something like this is going on when Galen, a late writer who sees himself as a Platonist, describes Medea:

> She knew that she was performing an impious and terrible deed . . . But then again anger like a disobedient horse which has got the better of the charioteer dragged her by force towards the children . . . and back again reason pulled her . . . And then again anger . . . and then again reason.

On this view Medea's final action is the result of a battle of forces in which the stronger wins, overpowering reason by brute force. This makes it much harder to see how Medea is in fact performing a deliberate action than it is if we accept the Stoic analysis. Epictetus thinks it obvious that Medea is acting in accordance with a deliberate view of what the best thing is for her to do; the problem is that this view is corrupted and malformed by anger. Given her resentment, what she did makes perfect sense; she is not overwhelmed, her reason drowned out.

Moreover, these different ways of looking at yourself make a difference to the attitude you take to other people who act under the influence of anger. Epictetus is sympathetic to Medea. Her view of what she should do was wrong – appallingly wrong – but we can understand it, and even sympathize with it, when we reflect that it is the response of a proud and dignified individual to a betrayal which refused to recognize her worth. We should pity Medea, says Epictetus; he certainly thinks that we can understand her point of view. Galen, by contrast, regarding her as overwhelmed by the animal-like part of the soul, sees her as animal-like, and like 'barbarians and children who are spirited by nature'. Medea is 'an example of barbarians and other uncivilized people, in whom anger is stronger than reason. With Greeks and civilized people, reason is stronger than anger.' (No prizes for guessing that Galen sees himself as a civilized Greek.)

Plato's view, then, is more complex than he realizes. It can lead in either of two very different directions: to seeing parts of myself as subhuman and not truly me, or it can lead to seeing them as junior partners with reason, either squabbling or making agreements. The second view is obviously much nearer to the Stoics.

Problems and theory

Plato and the Stoics see Medea in terms of very different accounts of human psychology and the emotions. So we find that the philosophical attempt to understand what is going on when we act because of emotion against our better judgement leads not to general agreement but to quite radical disagreement and to sharply conflicting conclusions. This is one reason why the example is an excellent introduction to thinking about ancient philosophy; for the tradition of philosophical thinking that developed in Greece and Rome is very often marked by strong disagreement and debate. Philosophical positions tend to be developed in dialogue and confrontation with other positions. Coming after Plato, the Stoics explicitly reject the idea of distinct parts to the soul; and Galen works out his own Platonist view in disagreeing with the Stoic view of the emotions. Philosophy in the ancient world was, with few exceptions, a way of thinking that developed in contested areas of discussion. Philosophers and their followers held, of course, that their own view was the true one, but they did not expect universal agreement; everyone was aware of the existence of rival, often equally prestigious positions.

What, then, does a philosophical explanation or theory do for us? We might think that we are no better off in understanding Medea after learning of the Stoic–Platonic dispute over the right way to interpret what is going on in her.

It is not so easy, however, to resist the search for a philosophical explanation of the phenomenon we are concerned with. I have chosen Medea as an example which was not only discussed in ancient philosophy but has continued to be a subject of lively concern in the modern world. If we look at artistic representations of the subject, or watch a performance either of Euripides' original play or of an updated version, we immediately see that a stand has to be taken on the Stoic–Platonic debate. Is Medea to be represented as overrun by passion which is overwhelming her power to reason what the best thing is for her to do? Or is she to be represented as a woman who is lucidly doing what she sees to be a terrible thing for herself as well as others, because she is not able to let go her ideals of pride and dignity?

Two nineteenth-century pictures of Medea bring out this point acutely. Eugène Delacroix's Medea is what Galen has in mind: a human overwhelmed by irrational feelings to the point of appearing radically non-human. Half-naked for no very obvious reason, her hair wild, her

1. Delacroix's Medea: a hunted animal

2. Sandys's Medea: deliberately choosing evil

vision symbolically shadowed, Medea writhes with her children in a dark cave, hunted like the animal she appears to be. Frederick Sandys's Symbolist picture, on the other hand, presents Medea as quite in control of what she is doing. Surrounded by the instruments of her revenge, which is just beginning, Medea is aware of, and troubled by, choosing the perverse course, but she is presented as reasoning in a controlled and deliberate way. The picture beautifies and aestheticizes revenge in a way distancing it from the Stoics, but it is still far nearer the Stoic than Galen's Platonic view.

There is no neutral way of presenting Euripides' *Medea*; directors and actors have to make fundamental decisions as to how she is to be represented, and they will be influenced by the translation or version used. This is one reason why she has remained a key case for discussion of reason and the passions. It seems, then, that any reflection about a case like this will reveal that we need to pursue philosophical explanation. But philosophical explanation is itself divided! How then can it advance us?

Philosophical explications of what is going on in a puzzling and difficult case may not leave us with a general consensus. (The more puzzling the case, the less likely this is to happen.) But we are driven to reflect philosophically about reason and passion for the reason already mentioned: until we try to understand what is happening, we are opaque to ourselves. If I act in anger, and reflect afterwards that I went against what I hold to be the best course, then I don't know why I acted as I did. If I accept Plato's theory, I will think of myself as internally divided, and my action as the result either of agreement between the parts of myself, or as the outcome of a battle between them (depending on whether I think of the parts other than reason as being themselves receptive to reasoning, or as non-rational, subhuman parts). If I accept the Stoic theory, I will think of myself as oscillating, as a whole, between different courses of action, motivated either by reasons of my overall good or by reasons infected by various

15

emotions. Either way I will understand more about myself and other people.

Philosophical understanding, in the tradition of ancient philosophy, is, as we shall see, systematic, part of a large theory. Plato's idea that the soul has distinct parts is worked out in different contexts in different dialogues. In the *Timaeus*, for example, he argues that the soul's parts are actually located in different parts of the body. In the *Republic* he draws an elaborate analogy between the parts of the individual's soul and the parts of an ideal society. The Stoic theory of the emotions is part of their ethical theory, and also part of the account they give of the role of reason in human life and in the world as a whole.

Most ancient philosophers see their task as being, in general, that of understanding the world, a task which includes understanding ourselves, since we are part of the world. Aristotle is the philosopher who puts the point most memorably: humans, he says, all desire by nature 'to understand'. The Greek word here is often translated as 'to know', but this can be misleading. What is meant is not a piling-up of known facts, but rather the achievement of understanding, something that we do when we master a field or body of knowledge and explain systematically why things are the way they are. We often begin looking for such explanations when we find things problematic, and Aristotle stresses that philosophy begins with wonder and puzzlement, and develops as we find more and more complex answers to and explanations for what were problems for us. We begin by being puzzled by the phenomenon of acting in passion against our better judgement; we understand it better when we have a theory which explains it to us in terms of a more general theory of human action. (Aristotle has his own theory on the topic, one distinctly closer to the Stoics than to Plato.)

What happens when I find that there are conflicting theories on the matter, and that holding one theory involves disagreeing with another? I am advancing further towards understanding, not retreating. For now it is

Aristotle (384–322 BC) Plato's greatest pupil, differs from him radically in method. He is a problem-centred philosopher, beginning from puzzles which arise either in everyday thinking or in the works of previous philosophers. He has a huge range of interests, producing work on a variety of topics, from formal logic (which he invented), to biology, literary theory, politics, ethics, cosmology, rhetoric, political history, metaphysics and much more. He is a systematic thinker, using concepts such as *form* and *matter* in a variety of philosophical contexts. However, his works (we have his lecture and research notes) aspire to system rather than achieving it. Later his work was systematized in often inappropriate ways (see pp. 93–5).

See the picture on p. 96.

clear that I have to put in some work for myself, in examining the different theories and the reasoning behind them – for I have to work out for myself which theory is most likely to be the right one. In the present case, it is clear that the Platonic and Stoic views can't both be right. Which is? Whatever I conclude, I have to be drawn into the theories and their reasonings. If I just feel that one appeals more than the other, but cannot back this up with argument, I have given up on my original drive to understand what is going on, to get beyond feeling puzzled and find some explanation. Ancient philosophy (indeed, philosophy generally) is typically marked by a refusal to leave things opaque and puzzling, to seek to make them clearer and more transparent to reason. Hence reading ancient philosophy tends to engage the reader's reasoning immediately, to set a dialogue of minds going.

Ancient philosophy is sometimes taught as a procession of Great

Figures, whose ideas the student is supposed to take in and admire. Nothing could be further from its spirit. When we open most works of ancient philosophy, we find that an argument is going on – and that we are being challenged to join in.

Chapter 2
Why do we read Plato's *Republic*?

Why do we read Plato's *Republic*? The question can point in more than one way. It could be asking for the point of reading this work – what we get out of it philosophically. Or it could be asking about the historical pressures of various kinds which bring it about that this, rather than some other, is the work we read. I might, for example, read it because it is part of a required course at university. Many people do just that. We do not read works of philosophy in a vacuum, and there are important, though far from completely understood, connections between the context of reading a work and what the reader will get out of it.

The first chapter introduced you to an issue in ancient philosophical debate which was (I hope) accessible without much adjustment. But not all issues in ancient philosophy are so easily available to a modern reader. In this chapter we will pull back the focus and look at some of the factors which separate us from ancient philosophical texts and issues. It is only when we confront these, as well as the factors making some ancient philosophy immediately engaging to us, that we will understand how we can read and argue with texts from such a distant and different culture.

The tradition and how it got to us

Before turning to the *Republic*, we need to think about the whole tradition of ancient philosophy, how it has come down to us, some of the changes that have occurred in our reception of it, and the way in which such changes can, for example, shape our reading of Plato and of a work like the *Republic*.

Ancient philosophy is, to begin with, a very large and rich tradition. It begins in the sixth century BC, and ends in the West with the end of the Western Roman Empire and in the East with the fall of the Byzantine Empire. It arose and developed in Greek city-states, especially Athens, but continued to flourish as the Romans dominated the Mediterranean and beyond, and formed an important part of culture in most of the Roman empire, merging into Christian culture with varied success. It forms a huge and extremely diverse body of texts. It contains a number of very different kinds of philosophical movements, from those that prize mystical insight and dogma to those that favour rigorous argument; a number of different and opposed schools, such as Stoics and Epicureans; and a range of wildly different philosophical positions, including materialism, dualism, scepticism and relativism. More will be said about these differences in Chapter 6; here I shall focus on factors in our reception of this tradition which make a difference to the way that ancient philosophy is seen as forming a tradition or canon, and to the way in which certain philosophers are seen as important.

Firstly, the issue of which parts of a tradition are seen as important only arises when we have the tradition. Much of ancient philosophy was lost to Western Europe in the period of the break-up of the Western Roman Empire, for a variety of reasons to do with cultural changes and the breakdown of political stability. Apart from Plato's dialogue *Timaeus*, for many hundreds of years the only ancient philosophical works which were known in depth were those of Aristotle, who dominated medieval philosophy. The period of the Renaissance saw the rediscovery, from a variety of sources, of a much wider range of ancient philosophers. But with the chances and fortunes of history, many ancient authors' original works have been lost, leaving us with only second-hand accounts of their theories and fragments of their own words. This is the fate of all the 'Presocratic' philosophers and of many philosophers after Aristotle, in the so-called Hellenistic period. Discoveries continue to be made of ancient philosophical works, mainly on papyrus rolls discovered in the dry sands of Egypt – and one collection of Epicurean works preserved in charred form at the eruption of Vesuvius. But big gaps remain, and for some individuals and schools of philosophy we remain dependent on often inadequate later accounts.

In AD 79 the eruption of the volcano Vesuvius covered in molten lava many aristocrats' country houses at Herculaneum, near Naples. This included one, which has been excavated since the eighteenth century, which turned out to contain a large library of books devoted to the works of the philosopher Epicurus and to later followers' discussions of his ideas. They lift the curtain on a hitherto unknown community of philosophical debate among Epicureans and with other schools. The books are rolls of papyrus (ancient paper), the charred fragments of which have been carefully studied by scholars.

Much of our evidence for ancient philosophy has a similarly accidental quality, and has come down to us in fragments.

Differences of approach

This situation opens up differences of approach. With authors whose work has to be studied in fragments and through later sources whose own approach has to be taken into account, historical and interpretative questions have to be faced before we can confidently assume that we actually have the philosophical position in question right. Wading right in with philosophical questions risks prematurely finding a position which turns out to reflect only our own philosophical concerns. It is more straightforward to approach authors whose own work we have as

3. A papyrus fragment of a work on anger by the Epicurean Philodemus

partners in a philosophical dialogue. It is not very surprising, then, that the authors whose philosophy is most prominently taught in philosophy departments are Plato and Aristotle, from whom we have complete works, rather than authors like Epicurus of whose original words we have only a small fraction.

This contrast can be overstated, however. Plato is the only author for whom we can feel certain that we possess all the works he made public. None of Aristotle's published works survive entire; what we have are his (very copious) research and teaching notes, which raise interpretative problems of their own. But even Plato is not a straightforward author to read; for one thing, the dialogue form distances the author from the ideas he puts forward, and interpretations of Plato are probably the most varied of any ancient philosopher. So it is just as possible to get Plato or Aristotle wrong by prematurely taking them to be engaged with our philosophical issues as it is with the Presocratics. And in any case authors and schools whose original work we have only in part can pose philosophical issues that engage us directly, despite the additional historical and interpretative work we have to do. The last twenty years has seen a huge shift in interest in research, publication and teaching in ancient philosophy, away from an almost exclusive focus on Plato and Aristotle to a concern with Hellenistic (post-Aristotelian) philosophers.

Changing interests

Why do we focus on one part of the many-faceted tradition of ancient philosophy rather than another? Apart from the vagaries of transmission, and the question of whether historical or philosophical interest is the driving one, there remains an ineliminable factor of philosophical interest, and this changes from period to period. Researchers and teachers are now interested in a wider range of issues and philosophers than they were twenty years ago, when Plato and Aristotle were more dominant; and similar shifts and changes have occurred many times in the past. Since there is no one single neutral way to take in, never mind discuss, the huge ancient tradition in full, this selectivity is not surprising. Nor should it surprise us that if we are introduced to one way of engaging with ancient philosophy, this should seem natural and inevitable, and that its limitations should become invisible, especially as it gets passed down from teacher to pupil and solidifies in books and journal articles.

We can, at least sometimes, trace an intellectual context to the way in which different parts of the ancient philosophical tradition are found interesting at different times. Some works of ancient philosophy seem dormant, as it were, at some times. They do not raise issues that people already find gripping, or ask questions to which people have competing answers. Then at other times they do do these things. Which parts of the ancient tradition that we engage with depend, at least to some extent, on our own philosophical interests. (How these, and changes in these, should be explained is another matter.) As we shall see, this is not a one-way street. Engaging with texts in ancient philosophy can help us to clarify and further our own thinking on some issues. (More on this in Chapter 3.) Because of their prominence in the teaching and development of Western philosophical thinking since the eighteenth century, some works of ancient philosophy form not just literally the ancient history of the subject, but part of the modern tradition too.

The changing fortunes of Plato's *Republic*

Plato's *Republic* is a dramatic example of the way a work of ancient philosophy can become, or cease to be, interesting to think about in contemporary philosophical terms. It is probably the most dramatic example.

For most of the twentieth century, and some of the nineteenth, the *Republic* has been far and away the best-known work of ancient philosophy. It is probably the only work in ancient philosophy that a large number of people have read. In universities, colleges and schools in many countries it figures in courses in ancient philosophy, in introductory philosophy, in 'Western Civilization', in political philosophy and in humanities. If you have to touch on ancient philosophy, or Plato, in any of these courses, the *Republic* is seen as the obvious work to choose. In modern readings of Plato the *Republic* is the centrepiece and high point of Plato's thought, the work which best presents the most important aspects of Plato's thought.

Plato's *Republic*

In the *Republic*, Plato tries to show that what makes a human life happy is to be found in being a good, virtuous person – something that the person has to achieve for herself, while wealth, status and other things commonly valued are irrelevant to happiness. This challenging thesis is defended by a claim that virtue consists in the proper ordering and structure of the person's soul, one in which reason rules (see Chapter 1). A properly ordered and so virtuous soul, compared to a properly ordered and so healthy body, brings the person a happy life, while unhappiness results from the breakdown of the soul's order. The framework of the book consists in Plato's developing and defending this idea that, contrary to popular belief, happiness is to be found in virtue, the right ordering of the soul, even in the worst possible conditions of poverty and torture.

As a model for the structure of the soul, Plato sketches the structure of an ideal society, with different kinds of people ordered in mutually beneficial ways, ruled by 'Guardians' who are devoted to the common good in the way that reason is devoted to the good of the whole person. Plato develops this devotion to the common good to extremes: Guardians will have no family life or private property, and much of their life will be devoted to training in the abstract metaphysical theory of 'Forms' (on this see below pp. 83–4). Strikingly, women as well as men will be Guardians – or, as they are sometimes called in view of their exacting philosophical education, 'philosopher-kings' (and philosopher-queens, of course).

This imaginative picture of an ideal society is developed further in narrative form in Plato's story of Atlantis, found in his *Timaeus* and unfinished *Critias*. The ideal society, projected back into history, is ranged against the exotic, romantic but corrupt society of Atlantis, an island in the middle of the Atlantic Ocean and later sunk there. This story, which Plato never finished, is probably his most influential contribution to literature outside the philosophical tradition.

There is another important point: the *Republic* is predominantly read in the light of its brief account of an ideal society. Plato there sketches an ideally just society, in which there would be complete division of labour between wealth on the one hand and political power on the other. The rulers would be 'Guardians', who would devote their lives to the public good and running the state. Those engaged in what we call economic activity would be excluded from political rule, on the grounds that their way of life narrows them to consider only their own self-interest and makes them unfit to take part in the public arena where what is at stake is the common good. The Guardian class, by contrast, is educated and trained to care primarily for the common good and to sacrifice their own interests to this.

It is often assumed that this ideal political construction is the organizing idea of the book; indeed often the book is introduced as though it were Plato's chief response to what he thought were political questions of the time. The *Republic* contains a number of themes. However, commonly what is seen as holding all these together is Plato's political vision, the idea that only in an ideal state, ruled in the interests of all, can people be virtuous and so happy. Sometimes this ideal of rule by the wise is seen as a reaction to the Athenian culture of democracy in which Plato grew up, and against which he reacted in what is assumed to be an élitist and reactionary spirit. So deeply ingrained is this way of reading the work that, at least in American libraries, the *Republic* and works about it are shelved in the political science section, rather than the history of philosophy section. The very way we have access to the book suggests the way we should read it. And it is often taken for granted that the book should be taught as a contribution to political thought, with its other aspects as extras.

But should we read the work this way? How else might it be read?

In the ancient world the *Republic* was read as one of Plato's dialogues, but by no means as the most important or as central for his thought. When philosophers began to study Plato's thought systematically, the dialogue they privileged was the *Timaeus*, a poetically written cosmology. What the *Republic* was mainly famous for was the idea that ideal rulers would have no private family life, but 'women and children would be in common', which was notorious, but was seen as eccentric rather than profound. Plato's political ideas in the work, while criticized by Aristotle, did not enter the mainstream of ancient political thought, although political ideas in other dialogues, the *Statesman* and *Laws*, did.

In the streams of medieval transmission of Plato's works the *Republic* was studied in the Islamic tradition, in which it was seen as suggestive of the idea of unified spiritual and secular power in ideal religious leaders. This idea did not develop in the Christian West; a tendency to think in terms of separation of church and state was aided by ignorance of the work until quite late. The work came into prominence at the Renaissance, and Italian thinkers who saw themselves as Platonists thought of it as an ideal Utopian fantasy. Throughout the seventeenth

27

and eighteenth centuries Plato fell into philosophical neglect, and the *Republic* was regarded as a mere oddity, if it was regarded at all. (See box, pp. 83–4).

Then, in the nineteenth century, Plato had a dramatic change of fortune, rising to the pre-eminence in study of ancient philosophy which he has kept ever since. The story of the rise of Plato in England is especially interesting, since there were three phases, each in response to a different philosophical approach.

The first English translation of the whole of Plato's works was made in 1804 by Thomas Taylor. Taylor was a self-educated man for whom Plato was a labour of love in a difficult life, so it is painful to have to say that the translations are awful. Taylor saw Plato's ideas in the framework of Neoplatonism, a later mystical elaboration of some of Plato's metaphysical ideas, and the result appealed to Romantic writers, but had influence on Wordsworth's poems rather than on philosophers.

The first concerted attempt to see Plato as a philosopher to whom argument matters was produced by the philosophers of the early nineteenth century that we call Utilitarians. This is quite surprising, since Utilitarian ideas about ethics and metaphysics are almost totally opposed to Plato's. Nevertheless, it was the circle of John Stuart Mill which revived the idea of Plato as a philosopher for whom arguments are what matter. The Utilitarian philosopher George Grote's *Plato* (1865), the first account based on solid scholarship, discussed every dialogue separately with its own theme and purpose, presenting Plato as engaged in an open-ended philosophical search, sometimes dogmatic and sometimes arguing against others without coming to a conclusion himself. Grote disagrees with Plato's ideas, but sympathetically presents him as following different arguments and directions. In this picture of Plato as essentially an argumentative searcher for truth the *Republic* appears as just one dialogue among many, containing some political ideas which are not seen as its centrepiece.

The Plato that won out, however, was a third Plato, the Plato of the Idealist philosopher Benjamin Jowett. Jowett translated all Plato's works (published in 1871) in a readable way that for the first time made Plato accessible to the general public. (We take translations for granted, but the *Republic* has been translated into languages such as Korean and Icelandic only in the last few years; when readers need to read Greek or to go through another language, Plato is accessible only to an educated élite.) Jowett saw Plato as a systematic thinker who points towards Idealism, and for him the *Republic* is central for the way in which he sees Plato bringing ethics and metaphysics together with politics. Moreover, he saw the political ideal as central, and in this he was followed by nearly everyone who has read the work since.

Why would Plato's ideal state seem like a serious contribution to political thought (as opposed to a Utopian fantasy)? By the middle of the nineteenth century political thinking was concerned with issues to which the *Republic* seemed relevant. Democracy and universal voting, long scorned as undisciplined mob-rule, had come to be a real political option, and the democratic city-states of ancient Greece came to replace the ancient Roman republic as a model in terms of which English and American politicians and political thinkers thought about their own states. Histories of ancient Greece began to present ancient democracy in a positive light for the first time. If the *Republic* could be seen as Plato's response to democracy then there were a number of contributions, negative and positive, that it could make to nineteenth-century political debate. And it was so seen.

Jowett made the *Republic* central to classical studies (a place it has retained ever since) and this idea of it as a serious, challenging and idealistic political text has spread all over the academic world. The nineteenth-century male élite who read the *Republic* at university were supposed to be inspired by it to adopt an ideal of selfless devotion to the public good, an ideal which was to serve as an antidote to economic ambition, which was seen as selfish. The idea of Guardians was seen as meritocratic: political rule should be earned by education and hard work, not inherited as an aristocratic privilege. Plato's idea of women Guardians was useful as the expression of an ideal, reflection on which would enable men to absorb the idea of women as political equals in society, entitled to the vote and to education. (Here we find Victorian anxiety about sex entering: Jowett goes to great lengths to separate female Guardians from Plato's ideas about 'women and children in common'.) Plato's insistence on a common system of public education for citizens was seen as an inspiration for the growing movement to democratize and spread education, and to see it as the state's task to provide it. Plato's complaints about democracy and his view that governing requires specialized knowledge were taken up in the ongoing debates about modern representative democracy and extensions of voting rights. The *Republic* provided materials for thinking about contemporary issues, and nineteenth-century concerns lit up Plato's ideal state as the controlling idea of the book.

Jowett's interpretation of the *Republic* has had an astonishingly long life. In English-speaking countries, it has long outlived the vogue for Idealist philosophy, and the political debates, that produced it. Even today it is often assumed that the obvious way to read the book is as an idealist political statement, in which questions of metaphysics and ethics are developed within the framework of the ideal state. Scholars have differed on how 'practical' the ideas are meant to be: some have seen them as merely an ideal to inspire, others as a blueprint to put directly into practice. And during the twentieth century the general reaction to the work has changed around completely from respectful to hostile. The political battles of the Victorian era being over, the *Republic* has been brought into relation with darker, more modern ideas. From the 1930s, the Guardians have been seen as a totalitarian, sometimes fascist idea, and Plato's insistence on common public education and culture has been claimed to be propaganda and brainwashing. (This idea was introduced to taint Plato by association with pre-war Nazi Germany, but has proved just as serviceable in associating him with post-war Communist régimes.

Is the *Republic* a political blueprint?

'Is not the Republic the vehicle of three or four great truths which, to Plato's own mind, are most naturally represented in the form of the State? . . . Through the Greek State Plato reveals to us his own thoughts about divine perfection, which is the idea of good – like the sun in the visible world; – about human perfection, which is justice – about education beginning in youth and continuing in later years – about poets and sophists and tyrants who are the false teachers and evil rulers of mankind – about "the world" which is the embodiment of them – about a kingdom which exists nowhere upon earth but is laid up in heaven to be the pattern and rule of human life . . . We have no need therefore to discuss whether a State such as Plato has conceived is practicable or not . . . For the practicability of his ideas has nothing to do with their truth.'

Benjamin Jowett, Introduction to his translation of the *Republic*

'The philosopher-king is Plato himself, and the *Republic* is Plato's own claim for kingly power.'

Karl Popper, *The Open Society and its Enemies*, vol 1.

Nowadays, although the wilder and sillier accusations of fascism have been discredited, few teachers put forward the *Republic* as containing positive ideas to emulate and inspire. It is far more often put forward as an objectionable, élitist and exclusionary set of political ideas which students who are brought up to be tolerant and inclusive can easily criticize without exerting themselves. Still, the underlying assumption remains unchanged, that the main thing the book is doing is putting forward an account of an ideal political community whose structure and organization provide an answer to genuine questions of political debate.

The political ideal of the *Republic*

'Plato is not an idealist, and the organic theory of society, as well as political totalitarianism, are altogether foreign to his thought. The human community, as he conceives it, is neither a mere juxtaposition of atomic individuals nor a superorganism living its own life apart from the individual members. It is rather a group of individuals unified by a shared purpose capable of eliciting co-operative acts.'

John Wild, *Plato's Modern Enemies and the Theory of Natural Law*

'I believe that Plato's political programme, far from being morally superior to totalitarianism, is fundamentally identical with it.'

Karl Popper, *The Open Society and its Enemies*, vol 1.

It has been so useful in this role, and productive of so much philosophical engagement, that it is easy to overlook the point that the interpretation of the *Republic* as centrally political theory is a Victorian one, and that we no longer share the Victorians' reasons for finding the work an evocative political model. We can see this by reflecting on the wide variety of mutually conflicting interpretations of the book that have been produced since the nineteenth century. The political interpretation has carried on, now partly because, as a work of political philosophy, the work is easy to criticize. Hence it has been treated as a teaching tool, providing an easy target for effortless demolition. But now that evaluations of the work have run the gamut, increasingly many scholars are looking at the foundations of the interpretation itself.

Questioning the context and arguing with the text

Is the *Republic* a political work? This is too complex a question for a quick answer, but, now that you have seen that the political interpretation has a very recent particular source, you may well want to ask yourself how (if you have read the book) you were encouraged to read it, and why. You may want to go back to the text and ask for yourself whether the way you were encouraged to read it was the best way.

One very obvious point about the *Republic* is that the description of the ideal state takes up only a small part of the work. It is far too brief and sketchy to be a 'blueprint' for political action, and it does not give the work its framework. The main argument of the book is posed at the beginning of the second book and answered at the end of the ninth, and it consists of Plato's attempt to answer the question, 'Why should I be moral?' Morality, it seems, benefits others rather than myself; would it not be better for me to live a kind of life in which I pursue my own ends in a way which ignores or exploits others? Plato thinks that a life in which morality is supreme can be rationally defended as the best life for an individual, even in the worst possible circumstances of the actual world. To make out his case, he introduces the ideal state as a parallel for the structure of the moral person's soul; as he says at the end of the argument, the ideal state shows us the abstract structure which the moral person takes as an ideal to internalize in his aspiration to live a good life. But the ideal state is not the idea which structures the *Republic*, and the questions Plato asks about the actual world cannot be answered by reference to an ideal state without breaking the back of the work's argument.

This is obviously only the beginning of an account of the work's overall plan. You may want to ask yourself just what work the ideal state does in illuminating the structure of the individual's soul. How serious are the political ideas, by comparison with those in Plato's political discussions in the dialogues *Statesman* and *Laws*? Most radically, you may want to ask whether introducing an ideal state into an argument about individual morality was one of Plato's better ideas. It has certainly been one of his more suggestive ones.

Why has the *Republic* been seen so often since the mid-nineteenth century as primarily a work of political theory? It is obvious that to some extent the Victorians, and subsequent generations, have used the *Republic* to develop their own ideas, and have read into the work what was necessary to do this. Plato's Guardians have been seen as meritocratic officials by Victorians worried about creating a more just society. They have been seen as fascist Big Brothers by twentieth-century thinkers worried about totalitarian states. But if the *Republic* can be used to come to such opposed conclusions, can we find a single political philosophy in it at all?

This can be a depressing thought. It can encourage the reflection that there is no real basis for an objective interpretation and assessment of the book, that each generation, or perhaps each reader, invents their own *Republic*, or at least the political philosophy in it. Outside academic post-modern circles, this is seen as a pessimistic conclusion to draw. The book certainly seems to be saying something which different readers with diverse concerns can argue about. It presents itself as a work of philosophy, encouraging us to make use of rational arguments and discussion as a way of arriving at the truth.

We can see the wild divergence of interpretations of the *Republic* not as a reason for lapsing into relativism about interpreting it, but as a sign of the richness and depth of the work. Even if, from Jowett onwards, the political content of the work has been grossly inflated, the result has been a lively and creative engagement with the text, at the end of which we can look back and see how much or little there is to the development of various lines of thought in the text. We can admire the way that the *Republic* has entered into, and been used to further, many nineteenth- and twentieth-century political discussions. It is the best example of the way in which engaging with a work of ancient philosophy can be a two-way street; bringing it into a discussion can enrich that discussion, while also encouraging us to see the work in the light of that discussion.

It is easy to see the changing fortunes of the *Republic* as a cautionary tale: what happens when a work of ancient philosophy is used as something 'good to think with' in a way that cuts it from its moorings, namely Plato's work as a whole, and the way it was received and studied until recently. But we can also more open-mindedly draw the lesson that we should be aware of at least three things when we study a work of ancient philosophy. One is our interest in seeing and engaging with the work in its own intellectual context. Secondly, our own assumptions as to what is philosophically salient and interesting, what we are likely to find intellectually rewarding. And thirdly, the potential of the work we study to engender creative philosophical thinking on our part. These factors may be of different strengths and come into play in different ways. One thing we can certainly learn from the history of reading the *Republic* is that lack of awareness of these factors can lead to fruitless wrangling over which of various mutually contradictory interpretations is the correct one.

If we think of the results of Chapter 1, we can see that sometimes an issue in ancient philosophy is part of an argument that we can immediately relate to. But we can now also see that there are potential dangers in this attitude. We should also be on the lookout for ways in which our own changing philosophical interests play a role in establishing what we find philosophically interesting in the ancient tradition. The *Republic* is the most extreme example of how a work can be moved from marginal to central, and from being an ethical work to being a political one, under the pressure of changed interests in the audience. The moral is not that we should think that our own interpretations of the *Republic* are nothing but reflections of our own prejudices. Rather, we should be aware of our own philosophical interests and the role they play, in order to lessen the extent to which they influence us unconsciously. While some parts of ancient philosophy seem extremely alien to our interests, others are too familiar. Sometimes we need to distance them from present concerns and ask about our traditions of interpreting them.

Engaging with ancient philosophical thinking may in Chapter 1 have sounded easy; now it may sound more difficult. With many texts, particularly the most famous ones, like Plato's *Republic*, the right approach is surely to think of them both as available to read and argue with, and as being in their own right the subject of a long tradition of engagement that we stand at the end of. It is, after all, what we would expect. When we begin to read ancient philosophers we feel like the first discoverers, but we soon find out that we are separated from them not merely by two thousand years but by many traditions of reading and writing about them. In recognizing the factors that separate us from the ancients, and that make the 'canon' of texts that we engage with so changeable, we bring philosophical discussion with them closer, rather than further away.

Chapter 3
The happy life, ancient and modern

You need to choose

A familiar story to anyone who had studied philosophy in the ancient world is Prodicus' Choice of Heracles. Prodicus was a so-called 'sophist' or professional intellectual of the fifth century BC. We have the story from a later writer, Xenophon, who recounted conversations of the philosopher Socrates.

Socrates is talking to a friend, Aristippus, who believes in going for what you want when you want it and not deferring your gratifications. Socrates objects that as a policy this may be dangerous; if you are unable to control your desires you may end up at the mercy of people who can, and who use their superior self-mastery to compete with you successfully and to gain control over your life. Aristippus doubts this. He can, he says, lead a life which is devoted to self-gratification and yet manage to avoid being dominated by others; and this is the way to happiness.

Socrates disagrees. It isn't, he thinks, just a matter of evading what others can do to you. It's a matter of how you regard your own life. To make the point he tells Prodicus' story of how the demi-god Heracles, at the start of adult life, came to a crossroads. Two women came along, each urging him to take one of the opposing ways. One was self-

The sophists

'Sophists' is the term used for a number of intellectuals in the fifth century BC who, while they did not form a unified intellectual tradition, represented a new departure. They travelled around various cities, teaching for money a variety of intellectual skills, the most saleable being skills in rhetoric and argument which would give the learner an advantage in public life. Although only some of their concerns fit into the philosophical tradition, they have remained on its edge because Plato immortalized them in many of his dialogues as pompous incompetent fools, a foil to his own hero Socrates. Plato's depiction is gleefully unfair, but we lack enough independent evidence to counter it in any detail.

The most famous sophists were Hippias of Elis, Prodicus of Cos, Thrasymachus of Chalcedon and Protagoras of Abdera. Hippias was famous for the large number of his accomplishments and Prodicus for his study of language. Thrasymachus is portrayed in the *Republic* as holding an account of justice which aggressively reduces it to the interest of the stronger. Protagoras is the only one who held an important philosophical thesis, namely relativism, the view that for a belief to be true is just for it to appear true to the person who holds it. Plato refutes this view in his dialogue *Theaetetus* (see p. 73 below).

Plato despises the sophists for many reasons. He rejects their views, particularly relativism, and he thinks that teaching intellectual skills for money debases these by turning them into commodities, valued for what they do for you rather than respected for their own sake. He also thinks that, just because they do not take it seriously, the sophists are in fact incompetent at philosophical argument. In his presentation of them, of course, they certainly are.

consciously fashionable, bold and made-up; she ran ahead of him and urged him to take the easy road of satisfying desires and going through life doing what he wanted, deliberating only as to how to do so with least effort. My friends, she said, call me Happiness, though my enemies call me Vice (or Pleasure). The other woman, solemn and modest in manner, appealed by her words rather than her appearance, and urged him to follow her, Virtue, even though her way was one of effort and frequent frustration rather than easy success. What I offer, she said, is worth while but requires work and self-denial; vice and pleasure offer an easy road to happiness, but the initial appeal fades and leaves you with nothing worth having, whereas virtue is the way to achievement and respect, which forms real happiness.

The Choice of Heracles forms a frequent subject in western art. The version illustrated here, by Paolo de Matteis, was commissioned in 1712 by the philosopher Anthony Ashley Cooper, third earl of Shaftesbury, to provide an illustration for his own book on virtue. It and many similar depictions reinforce something that makes a modern reader uncomfortable: moral choice is depicted as two females competing for a man. Moreover, even though one point is that what matters is reality, not appearance, this point is itself expressed in terms of one female being, on due consideration, more attractive than the other.

But apart from this, we may feel puzzled as to why this story, which seems to us over-obvious, should be famous. Clearly, we may think, if you are asked to choose between virtue and vice, you should choose virtue, but that's the easy part; the hard part is working out what virtue is, and depicting it as a modest maiden rather than a shameless floozy not only is a sexist way of presenting it, but doesn't help us much. If we think this, it is probably because much twentieth-century ethical thinking has made the ancient ethical framework unfamiliar. But this is a comparatively recent development, and one now rapidly being reversed, as virtue becomes more familiar in both philosophical and

4. Heracles deciding between austere Virtue and tempting Pleasure

political discourse. We are now, it turns out, in quite a good position to appreciate the claims of Virtue on Heracles.

Virtue and Vice are offering Heracles differing roads to happiness. Prodicus was one of the first philosophers to make explicit something important; we are all, in our lives, aiming at happiness. We find the thought also in the slightly later philosophers Democritus and Plato; the latter stresses that it would be ludicrous to deny that happiness is our overall goal in life, the destination on everyone's road.

But Prodicus also made a mark by emphasizing something else. When you are starting out on adult life, aiming at happiness, and doing so consciously, you will be faced with a *choice*. You can't have it all; you can't go through life gratifying your desires and still hope to achieve anything worthwhile or to live a life that you or others can respect. Recognizing explicitly that your aim in life is happiness brings with it the realization that you have to reflect on and order your life in one way rather than another. Life presents you with the alternatives; you have to make the decisions. Centuries later Cicero, aware of much sophisticated discussion, still thought that the story said something profound about everybody's life and their attitude to it.

Happiness and Pleasure

In the different tellings of the story the shameless floozy is indifferently Vice or Pleasure. In our traditions of moral philosophy it may seem strange that pleasure is the bad, rejected way of getting happiness. John Stuart Mill, a major founder of the Utilitarian tradition, actually defined happiness as pleasure and the absence of pain, but even if we do not see happiness as actually constituted by pleasure it still seems somewhat odd to see happiness as achieved by virtue *as opposed to* pleasure. Here we can see that ancient ethical thought gives a different conceptual role to happiness.

41

Happiness in ancient ethical thought is not a matter of feeling good or being pleased; it is not a feeling or emotion at all. It is your life as a whole which is said to be happy or not, and so discussions of happiness are discussions of the happy life. It is our bad luck that for us what is happy are not just lives, but also moments and fleeting experiences; modern discussions of happiness tend to get confused very rapidly because such different things are being considered. In ancient ethics happiness enters ethical discussion by a very different route from the 'feel-good' one.

Sometimes you step back from your routines of daily life and think about your life as a whole. You may be forced to do this by a crisis, or it might be that passing a stage in your life, such as becoming an adult rather than an adolescent – as in the Heracles story – makes you think about what you are doing in your life overall, what your values are and what matters most to you. For the ancients this is the beginning of ethical thinking, the entry-point for ethical reflection. Once you become self-aware, you have to face choices, and deal with the fact that certain values, and courses of action, exclude others. You have to ask how all your concerns fit together, or fail to fit. What you are looking for, all ancient thinkers assume, is how to make sense of your life as a whole, by bringing your concerns under the heading of your final aim or goal, your *telos*. For someone who fails to unify her concerns in any overall way is radically in denial about the way all her projects are hers, fit together in *her* life.

What can you say about the way your life is tending, the values you are expressing in your life? At first, probably not much. It is only after thinking through some ethical theories that you will have much of an explicit idea as to what values are unifying your life. But there is one thing that you can say, even before venturing on to theory: as philosophers from Prodicus on agree, and as is most famously set forth by Aristotle, everyone agrees that their final end is happiness, and that what people seek in everything they do is to live a happy life. (Hence ancient ethical theories are called eudaimonist, from *eudaimonia*, the Greek for happiness.)

Why is this supposed to be so obvious? It would not be obvious at all if happiness were introduced via the notion of pleasure or feeling good. But happiness answers to *formal* properties that our final end has. That is, the happy life has to meet certain demands before we can even start asking what its content is; any candidate for being the content – virtue, pleasure or whatever – has to meet these demands. The overall end which unifies all your concerns has to be *complete*: everything you do or go for is sought for the sake of it, while it is not sought for the sake of anything further. It also has to be *self-sufficient*: it does not leave out any element in your life that has value as part of living well. These are common-sense points, though they have powerful implications. And on the level of common sense or intuition, happiness is the only aim, plausible as an aim in your life as a whole, which is complete and self-sufficient. We do other things in order to be happy, but it makes no sense to be happy for some further reason. And once we are living happily we lack nothing further to be living well. These points are obvious with the ancient conception of happiness. But, as Aristotle immediately points out, they do not settle very much, for great disagreement remains as to how happiness should be specified, and the different schools of thought about ethics take off from here.

One point is clear right from the start, however. Happiness is having a happy life – it applies to your life overall. Pleasure, however, is more naturally taken to be something episodic, something you can feel now and not later. It is something you experience as you perform the activities which make up your life. You can be enjoying a meal, a conversation, even life one moment and not the next; but you cannot, in the ancient way of thinking, be happy one moment and not the next, since happiness applies to your life as a whole.

Hence we can see why Pleasure's role in Prodicus' story is to provide an obviously faulty road to happiness. Pleasure fixes us on the here and now, the present desire which asks to be satisfied; and this gets in the way of the self-control and rational overall reflection which is required by a life devoted to things that are worth while. Pleasure is short-term, while happiness is long-term. So, in complete opposition to the modern way of looking at the matter, it looks as though pleasure is not even in the running to be a candidate for happiness. How could your life as a whole be focused on a short-term reward like pleasure? Someone who does this is making a big mistake, giving in to the present satisfaction at the cost of a proper concern for the rest of his life.

In fact hedonism, the view that pleasure is our ethical end, is always on the defensive in ancient ethics. Opponents like to make it appear as though this is because there is something inherently unworthy about humans going for pleasure, but this is edifying rhetoric. The problem is rather that pleasure is defective as an aim that could structure a person's entire life. We can see this in the two major hedonist theories.

Aristippus founded a school called Cyrenaics after their home at Cyrene in North Africa. It was not a very unified school, but they all held that our final end – namely what we seek in everything we do – is pleasure, and by pleasure they uncompromisingly meant what we experience when we enjoy or feel good about some experience. Pleasure is a movement, not a settled state (and so is pain). Pleasures do not differ from one another, and one pleasure is not more pleasant than another; that is, pleasure is taken to be a single kind of experience which is always the same whatever the circumstances which produce it. We have access to pleasure only by our direct experience of it, and we have knowledge only of our experiences, not of the objects which produce them. Hence past pleasures, which have vanished, and future pleasures, which are still to come, cannot be compared with the present pleasure which we experience, and the Cyrenaics sometimes speak as though only the present exists; certainly the present is all that matters, and our lives should be so shaped as to get present pleasure.

Kinds of hedonism

Aristippus of Cyrene in North Africa (c.435–355BC) went to Athens and was an associate of Socrates. Evidence about his life is unreliable, consisting mainly of anecdotes showing him living a colourful life devoted to gratification, with no care for his dignity or for other people. However, he cared enough about his daughter, Arete, to teach her his ideas, and she passed them on to her son, Aristippus the Younger, who may be the source of the systematic philosophy attributed to the school of Cyrene.

Epicurus of Athens (341–270 BC) developed his own version of hedonism in a way that he represented as self-taught, although he did have some philosophical education. Around 307 he set up a philosophical school in Athens. Unlike the schools of Plato, Aristotle and the Stoics, it was not one which met in a public place and in which teaching prominently included argument and debate. Epicurus' school was called the Garden after its home, and his teaching put a premium on learning and memorizing the words of Epicurus and other founding members. Discussion took place orally and in writing throughout the school's history, but Epicureans regarded Epicurus as a saviour from unhappiness and a shining light in a way that philosophers from other schools found too deferential. Epicurus' main contribution was his hedonistic ethics; in his philosophy of nature he took over the views of the earlier Atomist Democritus, developing a world-view in which, unusually in ancient philosophy, there is no room for providence or teleology of any kind, and the gods, though they exist, take no interest in the world or in human beings.

If all that matters is to get present pleasure, what has happened to happiness? Alone among ancient philosophers, some of the Cyrenaics say that we should not be concerned about it. A happy life is an organized one in which past and future pleasures count in relation to present ones, but if our concern should always be to pursue the present pleasure then happiness will often get in the way of this, and we should disregard it.

This might sound like a suicidal strategy for living your life, one that is bound to favour short-term production of intense present pleasure from, for example, sex and drugs, with no thought for your future. In fact the Cyrenaics do not have to hold this; they only have to hold that reflection on and concern for your life as a whole has value only insofar as it tends to produce present pleasure. This means that overall reflection about your life can have value only instrumentally, as a means to something else. This thought seems to have been found deeply unpersuasive; at any rate the Cyrenaics were never more than an eccentric school in ancient ethical thought.

Epicurus seems to have learned from their failure, and he makes an effort to present pleasure as a candidate for happiness that meets the overall demands, thus making his theory more acceptable and mainstream. Your concern with your whole life, he thinks, is not just a means to enjoyment of the present; rather, it matters to you in its own right, as people commonly think. However, the happy life is, in fact, a life of pleasure.

We can see from the moves already made that this is going to sound strange: how can focusing on short-term gratifications *also* be a long-term concern with what matters overall in your life? Epicurus has to deny that pleasure is always short-term enjoyment. There are two kinds of pleasure, he insists, and while one of them is the kind of enjoyment that people get from activities such as eating, drinking, sex and the like, and is a 'movement', there is also another, 'static' kind, and *this* is what we should be seeking as the right way of achieving the happy life. Static pleasure is the absence of bodily pain and mental trouble; it is the state where you are functioning without impediment or discomfort. Epicurus boldly claims that this state is the highest pleasure that we can achieve – that is, you achieve happiness not by doing things that make you feel good, but by so ordering your life that you achieve this condition of painlessness and tranquillity. Unsurprisingly, doing this involves 'sober reasoning', which scrutinizes your life carefully and rejects activities which will result overall in impingements on your tranquillity. Hence short-term gratification and success is rejected if the results will lead to a less balanced and undisturbed plan of life overall. The Epicurean happy life, then, far from being a wild pursuit of fun experience, turns out to be a cautious and risk-aversive strategy for maintaining tranquillity. Critics did not tire of pointing out that, even if this is an acceptable idea of living happily, it is a peculiar conception of the most *pleasant* way we could live.

We can see why, given the ancient framework for ethics, hedonism is at a disadvantage. Hedonists seem condemned to giving an implausible account either of happiness, as with Aristippus, or of pleasure, as with Epicurus.

Our modern conception of happiness is frequently understood in terms of pleasure and desire-satisfaction (something aided by the wide and confused way we use 'happy'), and this can make it hard at first to see the appeal of ancient theories of happiness. If happiness is just getting what you want, then the ideas in the Choice of Heracles make no sense. However, our ideas about happiness derive from many sources and also contain elements more congenial to eudaimonism. We think of a happy life as involving achievement and success, for example, rather than just getting what you want. Theories of happiness as desire-satisfaction systematically run into problems once we face them with thoughts about our life as a whole.

Happiness and Virtue

Until recently, though, the really alien idea in the Choice of Heracles would have been thought to be the role of Virtue. In modern ethical thought, until quite recently, virtue had become something of a joke concept, one that could be understood only historically and could not be seriously used in ethical thinking. In the last decade, however, 'virtue ethics' has had a spectacular comeback. Once again, however, we find that there is not a perfect match between our notion of virtue and the ancient one, and so some explanation and comparison is needed.

A minimal conception of ancient virtue is that of having a systematic concern to do the morally right thing. All that this assumes is that we have some grip on the idea of doing what is morally right, as opposed to what is wrong. We do not have to start with an elaborate theory as to what is morally right; our account of this is deepened as the account of virtue develops.

Virtue is a richer notion than this, but already it is distinguished from non-moral concerns – the idea, for example, that virtue is a sort of non-moral 'excellence'. (Unfortunately, a misguided attempt to 'modernize' ancient ethical texts has led some translators to render the Greek word *arete* by 'excellence' rather than the supposedly old-fashioned 'virtue', thus obscuring the point that the texts are about morality. This is especially unfortunate now that modern moral philosophers are recognizing the moral import of virtue.)

Someone wanting to be prepared to do the morally right thing, not just occasionally but systematically, will have to have developed self-mastery and strength of mind to overcome the (very many) incentives we have to do something else. Hence it is not surprising that Virtue tells Heracles that her way is difficult and often unpleasant and frustrating. It is fine to do the morally right thing, but the virtuous person has to do a lot more than that. She has to develop a disposition, a firm state, of doing the morally right thing. And to get to that point she has to have developed two things, a firm understanding of morality and the willingness to act on it. Neither is easy or rapidly developed, and by the time someone is virtuous he will have made himself be a certain kind of person. Hence there is a connection between virtue and your life as a whole: becoming virtuous is becoming a person with a certain kind of *character*, and this requires reflecting in a thoughtful way about your life as a whole and the kind of person you aspire to be, as well as having the motivation to follow through on this. Neither is going to happen if you simply go along satisfying your desires and never developing the ability to think and act in the long term.

The modern conception of virtue is in many ways weaker than this. A virtue is often thought of as a kind of habit of acting in a certain way; this makes the virtues look like separate habits which grow up in locally isolated ways, since it certainly seems that you can develop a habit of generous giving without having a habit of acting bravely. In the ancient way of looking at it, isolated habits of action have to be unified by your understanding of what is morally appropriate, since it could hardly be the case that morality made one set of requirements for generosity and another, quite unrelated set for courage. In ancient ethics the point is not to have localized virtues but to be virtuous, to have the unified understanding which grounds all the virtues and is called practical wisdom or *phronesis*.

The ancient conception of virtue, moreover, is one in which practical wisdom takes the form of practical reasoning which is integrated with the motivation to do it. We have seen in Chapter 1 that there are many ancient theories as to the relation of reason and emotion; but all agree that in the virtuous person emotion and feeling are not, or are no longer, fighting against reason. The person who understands what the moral action requires, but has to battle down contrary motivation in order to do it, is not yet virtuous, but only self-controlled. Virtue requires that the person's motivation go along with her understanding.

Virtue, then, is a pretty demanding idea, in the ancient way of looking at it. It's not hard to see why critics of Epicurus' hedonism charged that he could not account for virtue. If pleasure is what we should be going for as our overall aim, then it is hard to see why we should care about the claims of morality except as means to gaining pleasure or avoiding pain. Epicurus denies that he is committed to this, but his critics seem to have the better of him here.

Can you be happy on the rack?

Most pressing, in ancient ethical debates, is the issue of the place of virtue in happiness. Virtue is the right pathway to the happy life, but this leaves many options open. Happiness is our overall aim, the goal for whose sake we do and seek everything else, while we don't seek to be happy for any further reason. Being a virtuous person will matter for this, but surely, we may think, common sense requires that other things matter too – for example, having a reasonable amount of money and other necessities, achieving success and so on. How could a happy life be a completely poverty-stricken and unsuccessful one?

Aristotle, who among ancient philosophers sticks most closely to common sense, agrees that this reaction of ours is an important one. Happiness, he holds, does require some amount of 'external goods' like money and success. On their own, no amount of such goods could make you happy, since whether or not you have them is not primarily up to you, and he thinks that, once you have begun to reflect ethically on your life, happiness must come from your own reflection on and organization of your life, and cannot just lie in external goods that circumstances can give and take away. Aristotle, however, fights shy of the idea that you can make yourself happy by making yourself virtuous. If that were so, he says, then a virtuous person would be happy even if he met with great and undeserved misfortunes, such as being tortured on the rack – and that would be hopelessly absurd.

Aristotle's conclusion tends to sound reasonable to us, since we have almost certainly never thought that being a virtuous or moral person is sufficient for having a happy life; so we can miss the point that in terms of the ancient theories it is a very unsatisfactory position to be in. He has to hold that the kind of person you are matters for having a happy life more than having money, status and so on, which matter only a certain amount; but he cannot say just how much they matter, since he is unwilling to say that a person who loses just that amount of money, status or whatever, is bound to be unhappy. Often he stresses that what is significant for living a happy life is not the goods you have but the use you make of them; just as the shoemaker does the best he can with whatever leather he has, and people who have suffered misfortunes do the best they can with what circumstances allow them. Hence he is unwilling to allow that a virtuous person who at the end of his life falls into great misfortune (such as Priam, the good king of Troy who lives to see his sons killed and city destroyed) must be considered to have lost their happiness. On the other hand, he wants to skirt what he sees as the ridiculous conclusion that the virtuous person is, just by being virtuous, happy whatever bad things happen to him. Hence he can allow neither that Priam after the fall of Troy is happy, nor that he is unhappy; he is torn between the common-sense view that of course he isn't happy, and the more theoretical idea that he has not lost his happiness, since happiness has to come from what you have made of your life, not from what other people do to you. So Aristotle's position is not really coherent – an irony, since he is the ancient philosopher most popular with and appealed to by modern authors developing theories of 'virtue ethics'.

Plato and the Stoics, more willing than Aristotle to discount ordinary views, defend the view that being virtuous *is* sufficient for a happy life. We can see that this is not, in the framework of ancient ethical thinking, the disastrously high-minded but implausible claim that it would seem if brought out without preface nowadays, but it may still seem unrealistic.

They think, however, that Aristotle makes a mistake in allowing that external evils subtract from the contribution to happiness that virtue makes. In fact, they think, virtue has a quite different kind of value. The Stoics put this point dramatically by saying that virtue is the only thing that *is* good, whereas health, money and so on should be called 'indifferent', although if we naturally go for something, such as health, it is a 'preferred indifferent'. They were not afraid to make themselves sound somewhat ridiculous by inventing new terminology disallowing straightforward computation that includes both virtue and external goods. In this respect they anticipate some of Kant's ideas about moral and non-moral value.

But is it just high-minded assertion that virtue is what matters most? Among the ways this is defended is the view, widespread in ancient ethics, that virtue is a kind of understanding of moral value (an understanding which, as we have seen, includes and is not opposed to affect and positive motivation), one that can be seen as an expertise or skill, exercised on the materials provided by the circumstances of your life. Just as a product or a work of art can be produced skilfully even with limited or inferior materials (something clearest in the performing arts) so a life can be well, and so happily lived even though the circumstances the person had to work on were inferior or positively bad. Aristotle comes near this idea when he compares the person in misfortune to the shoemaker doing the best he can with inferior leather; but he is too impressed by the idea that the product will be inferior to appreciate the point that the exercise of skill, the actual performance of the expert, may well be as impressive (or more so) in reduced circumstances as in good ones. The idea that virtue is a skill and that external advantages are its material makes prominent the idea that you make your own life; whatever you have to work with, the moral quality of your life comes from the way you live it, the choices you make and their implications for your character.

This idea is strikingly egalitarian, and accounts for the Stoic position

Can you be happy on the rack?

'[T]he happy man needs the goods of the body and external goods, i.e. those of fortune . . . in order that he may not be impeded . . . Those who say that the victim on the rack or the man who falls into great misfortunes is happy if he is good are, whether they mean to or not, talking nonsense.'

Aristotle, *Nicomachean Ethics*, Book VII, Chapter 13

'Aristotle's works on this, the *Nicomachean Ethics* and others, have ideas about virtue which are petty and grovelling and vulgar . . . they dare to grab from virtue the diadem and royal sceptre which she holds inalienably from Zeus. They do not permit her to make us happy, but put her on a level with money, status, noble birth, health, beauty and other things which are common to virtue and vice. Just as any of these without virtue is not sufficient to render its possessor happy, so virtue without these, they say, is in the same way insufficient to make its possessor happy. How, then, is the value of virtue not destroyed and overthrown?'

Atticus, second century AD Platonist

that happiness is attainable not just by those well-provided by life with money, good looks and status, but also by those who have bad luck: slaves, the conquered, people in limited social positions, like most women in the ancient world. It is notable that two of our major Stoic texts from the period of the Roman empire come from Marcus Aurelius, an Emperor, and from Epictetus, a freed slave. Stoicism was available equally to both of them as a philosophy to live by.

But if external goods do not contribute to our happiness, why should we even bother with them? The Stoic position here is subtle and hard to express briefly, but important here is the idea that we should make moral decisions from where we are. When you start to think about virtue, you are not a blank slate; you already have a given nature with needs for food, security, and so on, and also a social position: you already have a family, a nation, a job, and so on. It would be absurd, flouting human nature, to try to sacrifice or ignore these facts in the name of virtue; rather, we should aim to deal virtuously with them, always remembering that the demands of virtue trump them. Again, there are many affinities with Kant's moral thinking.

Virtue, ancient and modern

'Virtue ethics' has recently moved to the foreground of contemporary moral thinking, and with it an engagement with ancient ethical theories (unfortunately with a disproportionate emphasis on Aristotle). A common worry, which threatens to isolate the ancients from us, is that the development of a virtue is the development of a habit of doing the morally right thing – but what that is, is given by what virtuous people in your society do. Virtues develop within cultures and traditions; noticing this obvious enough point sometimes produces the charge that eudaimonist ethics is essentially conservative. Aristotle delineates the virtues recognized in *his* society; but these are the virtues of a privileged élite – free adult Greek males – and have dubious moral relevance beyond that, or to potential social improvements.

This common charge misses the point. Of course we begin by emulating the people we recognize as virtuous in our society; hence, unsurprisingly, virtues differ between cultures. But this is all prior to the beginning of ethical thought; ancient ethics begins at the point when the individual starts to reflect about her life as a whole, and make decisions which recognize the necessity of choosing between options, as Heracles does. The ancient ethical agent takes charge of his life; as practical reasoning develops he becomes ever more in control of it, and ever more responsible for the quality of it. Of course the result is different now from what it was in ancient Greece. How could it not be? The options are different. What is the same is the difference that is made when the agent stops drifting along in her life and taking for granted the social pressures on it, and starts to think ethically about it and the form it takes.

Ancient ethical thought is attractive because, among other things, it unites two concerns which are hard to find together in other traditions. One is a sense of the demands of morality, the recognition that morality makes a huge difference to all of your life. The other is a rootedness in concerns that we all have, and have difficulty making ethical sense of – family, jobs, commitments, friends, and the business of everyday living. The person who follows philosophy to the point of holding that virtue is sufficient for happiness has travelled a long way from her original concerns, and yet has never abandoned them.

Chapter 4
Reason, knowledge and scepticism

In Chapters 1 and 2 we saw how immediately gripping a topic in ancient philosophy can be, but also how we engage with the tradition in ways which reflect our own historical openness to some aspects rather than others. In Chapter 3 we explored an aspect of ancient philosophy – the ethical framework of virtue and happiness – which has turned out particularly fruitful for modern philosophical explorations. Now we shall look at some of the strands of ancient thinking about knowledge, and the lack of it, which on the face of it show more contrast than likeness to modern thinking on the topic.

Assumptions about knowledge

In modern epistemology, or theory of knowledge, certain assumptions are common. Among them is the view that the existence of knowledge must be justified against the sceptic, that is, the person who thinks that we can never know anything, because he holds that we can never meet the conditions for knowledge. Knowledge is taken to be, at least in part, a matter of being in the right relation to facts or information. (What is this right relation? Here we find very different views, which can barely be indicated here. Some philosophers stress justification, others the right causal connection, and there are sophisticated variants and combinations of these positions.) It is hard to imagine a modern epistemologist being impressed by the thought that your mechanic *knows* how to fix cars. It is equally hard to think of her finding it important that someone who knows lots of facts in science, say, may lack understanding of them. And what modern epistemologist would greet an authoritative pronouncement that she in fact possessed knowledge by trying to refute it?

We can start to understand what is distinctive about ancient attitudes to knowledge by beginning with Socrates. His friend Chaerephon, we are told, asked the oracle of the god Apollo at Delphi whether anyone was wiser than Socrates, and Apollo replied that nobody was. On being told this, Socrates was surprised, and wondered what the oracle could possibly mean, since he was aware that he possessed no wisdom or expertise of his own. So he went round people considered experts, questioning them about their alleged expertise, but always finding either that they could produce no remotely adequate account of what they were supposed to be experts in, or that the expertise they did have was less important than they thought it. He concluded that Apollo's meaning must be that the wisest person is the person most aware of their own ignorance.

Of all ancient philosophers, Socrates is the most recognizable. There is good reason for this; for ancient culture in general Socrates serves as the symbolic figure of the Philosopher. However, it is also remarkable, given that his life is elusive, he wrote nothing, and left a series of wildly differing philosophical legacies.

Socrates lived from about 468–399 BC. His father was a stonemason called Sophroniscus, his mother a midwife called Phainarete. His circumstances were initially prosperous, but by the end of his life he was poor, as a result of neglecting his practical affairs in his devotion to philosophy. His wife, Xanthippe, has an aristocratic name; she passed into legend as the shrewish wife of the undomestic philosopher, but we do not know what lies behind this. They had three sons, one young at the time of Socrates' death. Later, unreliable tradition ascribes to him a second wife, Myrto.

In 399 Socrates was tried and executed. The charges are strikingly vague and prejudicial, and it has always been suspected that the real agenda was political. We shall never know the facts. Clearly Socrates was widely regarded as an annoying and subversive presence in Athens.

Socrates identified the practice of philosophy with personal discussion and questioning, refusing to write anything. His followers elevated him to the founding figure of their mutually conflicting approaches to philosophy. Through his austere disciple Antisthenes, Socrates was regarded as the inspiration for the convention-rejecting Cynics; through his disciple Aristippus, he was claimed as the first hedonist. Through the tradition of Plato's Academy he was hailed as the first sceptic; through the Stoics he was regarded as the first ethical philosopher. In the writings of his younger follower Xenophon he appears as a conventional moralizer. In the writings of Plato, Socrates appears in a variety of guises. Sometimes he is the questioner who undermines the pretensions of others to understanding; sometimes he puts forward positive claims about ethics and metaphysics; sometimes he merely introduces other philosophers who have things of their own to say. Socrates continued to be influential as the figure of the philosopher par excellence, and his refusal to commit himself to authoritative teaching made him a usefully plastic figure whose influence could be claimed for widely different views and approaches.

This minimal construal of what a god means by calling a human 'wise' is in keeping with a Greek tradition of emphasizing the gulf between human and divine capacities. It also brings out some assumptions about ancient epistemology. Socrates goes round denying that he has knowledge, but this is never understood to mean that he does not know ordinary, everyday facts; he is aware of knowing large numbers of these. Further, he sometimes claims to know quite substantial pieces of moral knowledge, such as that he should never do wrong, or abandon what he regards as his divine mission. What he denies having is knowledge in the sense of wisdom or understanding, which goes beyond mere knowledge of isolated facts and is assumed to be found, if at all, in people who are experts in something. When Apollo says that he is the wisest person, then, Socrates is troubled by it, since if a person is an expert in something, he would normally be expected at least to be aware of what he is an expert in. He responds to the oracle by trying to find someone wiser than he is, then, not out of a rude desire to show

The trial of Socrates

'The following sworn indictment has been brought by Meletus, son of Meletus, of Pitthos, against Socrates, son of Sophroniscus, of Alopeke. Socrates does wrong in not recognizing the gods which the city recognizes, and in introducing other, new divinities. Further, he is a wrongdoer in corrupting the young.'

This indictment against Socrates was preserved in the archives of Athens and reported by later scholars. Socrates was found guilty by about 280 votes to 220. (Juries consisted of 501 citizens.) The prosecutor proposed death as a penalty. Socrates at first refused to allow that he had done anything deserving of a penalty, but eventually suggested a fine. The jury voted for death by a larger margin, about 360 to 140.

Apollo wrong, but because he does not understand the oracle, and the only way to find out how he is the wisest person is to find out what the expertise is which he is supposed to have. And, since this is obviously not self-declaring, the only way to find it out is to see how well he compares with other people in understanding what they are supposed to be wise about or experts in; and this can only be achieved by questioning them about what they are supposed to understand.

A number of points emerge in Socrates' response to the oracle. Philosophically interesting questions about knowledge are taken not to concern our relation to particular facts – how I can *know*, for example, that the cat is on the mat. Philosophical attention is focused on a more complex matter: the possession of wisdom (*sophia* – the wisdom loved by the *philosophos*). It is assumed, taken to be a matter beyond argument, that wisdom is not just knowing individual facts, but being able to relate them to one another in a unified and structured way, one that involves understanding of a field or area of knowledge. (A useful parallel is that of knowing a language, which obviously involves more than knowing individual pieces of information about vocabulary and syntax, and requires the understanding of how these fit together in a unified way. The language example also brings out the way that this unified understanding is not a theoretical grasp cut off from practice, but may itself involve a practical ability to apply the understanding in question.) The philosophically interesting kind of knowledge involves a complex of items grasped together in a way that enables the knower to relate them to one another and to the structure as a whole. In all but the simplest cases this grasp will require an articulate ability to do this relating, one which will explain why the different items play the roles they do in the system. (Think of teaching a language.) Such a grasp will typically be found in someone who has expertise (*techne*) in a subject.

Socrates never raises the question whether there is such a thing as wisdom or expertise. This would be silly, since there obviously are experts in some fields, such as crafts. Presumably, though, Apollo meant more than that Socrates had the kind of expertise to be found in weavers and potters, so Socrates' search is for expertise in matters of importance in human life. Hence he is particularly keen to question self-styled experts in virtue, or what is worthwhile in life, such as the sophists claimed to be. He questions them on the topics that they claim to be experts in, and always succeeds in showing that they lack

Differing views of Socrates

'Mankind can hardly be too often reminded, that there was once a man named Socrates, between whom and the legal authorities and public opinion of his time there took place a memorable collision . . . This acknowledged master of all the eminent thinkers who have since lived – whose fame, still growing after more than two thousand years, all but outweighs the whole remainder of the names which make his native city illustrious – was put to death by his countrymen . . . Socrates was put to death, but the Socratic philosophy rose like the sun in heaven, and spread its illumination over the whole intellectual firmament.'

John Stuart Mill, *On Liberty*

'Socrates – that clown from Athens!'

Zeno of Sidon, Epicurean philosopher, second century BC

'We shall ignore Chaerephon's story about the oracle, since it is an utterly sophistical and cheap trick.'

'Socrates, the arguments you worked out are bogus. The conversations you had with the people you met are one thing, and what you did was another.'

Colotes, early Epicurean philosopher, third century BC

5. The image of Socrates: physically ugly, intellectually an enchanter

understanding of these topics, since they fail to explain satisfactorily why they say what they do, and indeed often make inconsistent claims. Socrates' questions do not start from a position of his own, since this would only weaken the point that it is the other person who is supposed to display understanding of what *he* claims to know. When Socrates deflates the self-styled experts by showing them, just from premises that they accept, that they don't understand the subject they have been pontificating about, they cannot defend themselves by faulting his views, since these have not come into it.

Understanding and what it involves

What would show that a person has wisdom and understanding comes to be referred to as 'giving an account', *logon didonai*. *Logos* is the ordinary Greek word for reason; what you say about the topic you are supposed to understand must give reasons in a way that explains the matter. Socrates' victims can produce plenty of words, but they fail to give a reasoned account of their subjects, and so are shown not to understand what they are talking about.

What are the standards for 'giving an account'? This is obviously crucial for the question of whether you really know, that is, understand something. Minimally, of course, you have to be able to keep your end up in an argument and show that your position is consistent. But something more positive than this seems required too. One major strand of ancient epistemology consists of exploring the requirements for 'giving an account', providing the reasoned basis necessary if you are to have understanding of a field of knowledge.

In many of Plato's dialogues Socrates suggests that you have to be able to provide a satisfactory answer to the questioner who wants to know what virtue is, or courage, or friendship, or the like. This is obviously not provided by trivially appealing to the meaning of words; it has to express the nature of virtue, or courage, in such a way that the person

Reason, knowledge and scepticism

to whom it is successfully conveyed will be able not only to recognize examples of virtue, or courage, but to explain why they are examples of the virtue in question, relating them to its nature. This exploration is sometimes called a search for 'Socratic definitions', although 'definition' is an unhappy term here.

One standing puzzle about these dialogues is the following. Socrates is ambitiously searching for understanding of difficult concepts like virtue and courage. But his approach is always to question others, starting only from shared premises. This kind of *ad hominem* arguing relies only on what the opponent accepts and what it produces, time after time, are conclusions as to what virtue, courage, friendship and so on are *not*. Some self-styled expert makes a claim as to what virtue, etc. are, and Socrates shows that this cannot be the right answer. This does not, however, seem to move us towards understanding what virtue, courage and so on *are*. Socrates shows that others lack understanding, but not in a way that seems to be cumulative towards obtaining understanding of his own. There appears to be a mismatch between the goal and the methods. There are many ways of resolving this puzzle, and philosophers are divided over it.

Plato has a variety of concerns with knowledge, to some of which we shall return. Some of his most famous passages, however, show the dominance of what we can call the expertise model for knowledge. What is taken to matter for knowledge is whether you can, as an expert can, grasp the relevant items in a way that relates them to one another and to the field as a whole, and can give a reasoned account of this, one which explains the particular judgements you make and relates them to your unified grasp of the whole. And in some places Plato rethinks the crucial idea of giving a reasoned account, taking mathematics as his model.

In the *Republic*, Plato develops possibly the most ambitious model for knowledge that any philosopher has put forward. Now the aspiring knower has to complete an apprenticeship of many years' mathematical studies. Mathematics – by which he is primarily thinking of the kind of systematized geometry of which we have a later example in Euclid – is remarkable for its rigour, system and clarity. It struck Plato as a perfect example of the kind of structured body of knowledge that had been presupposed all along by the expertise model. Moreover, all the features of the expertise model seem to fit mathematics in a clear and impressive way. Mathematics is not a heap of isolated results; particular theorems can clearly be seen to depend on other results which are proved in turn. The whole system begins from a clear and limited set of concepts and postulates. The way in which we get from these first principles to particular results is also lucid and rigorous. It is easy to see why Plato might see in an earlier version of Euclid a splendid model of knowledge as a structured and unified system, one where it is absolutely clear what the knower knows and how she knows it, how the system holds together and what it is to give a reasoned account of what you know – namely, a proof.

Mathematics as a model for knowledge also introduces two new notes. One is that mathematical results are peculiarly unassailable; we do not waste time arguing that Pythagoras' theorem is wrong. We have seen that certainty and justification of what is known are not prominent in the cluster of issues that are the focus of the expertise model, where what matters is understanding that can be applied in practice. But Plato is clearly at some points attracted by the idea of a body of knowledge that is not open to serious questioning.

The other point flows from the fact that mathematics provides us with a body of firm knowledge which does not seem in any plausible way to have as its object the world that we experience, in an everyday way, through the senses. Pythagoras' theorem was not discovered by measuring actual drawn triangles and their angles, and irregularities in these are obviously irrelevant to it. Plato is attracted to the view that a body of knowledge can exist to which our access is solely by using our minds and reasoning. He is not the last philosopher to be tempted by the view that the powers of philosophical reason are more developed versions of our ability to reason mathematically.

In the *Republic*'s central books, we find that to have knowledge requires mastery of a systematic field whose contents are structured as rigorously as the axioms and theorems in Euclid, and linked by chains of proof. Moreover, Plato goes one better than the mathematicians in claiming that philosophy actually proves its own first principles – something which mathematicians fail to do – and so does not begin from assumptions, but shows how everything flows from a first principle which is proved and not assumed. (Here matters get obscure, particularly since Plato makes everything depend on what he calls the Form of the Good.) As with mathematics, what is known is a formal system – what Plato famously regards as the world of Forms – and not the world of experience revealed to us by the senses; indeed, Plato goes out of his way to stress the extent to which the person thinking in abstract mathematical terms will come to conclusions at odds with experience.

This is, of course, an *ideal*, something emphasized by the way that the only people who, Plato thinks, have a chance of attaining it are those who are exceptionally talented by nature and have been brought up in ideal cultural circumstances. This warns us against thinking that we can find any actual example of knowledge. The expertise model on its own seemed to hold out the chance at least that knowledge was attainable. But when the requirements are made as formal and demanding as they become when mathematics is the model, the conditions for knowledge get set so high as to be unattainable by us.

Understanding and the sciences

Aristotle, in this as in many matters Plato's greatest pupil, takes over the *Republic* model, but with important modifications which make it philosophically far more fruitful. He develops the idea in his work on the structure of a completed body of knowledge, the unfortunately titled *Posterior Analytics*. (It is so called because it follows his treatise on logic, the *Prior Analytics*.)

For Aristotle, Plato goes wrong in thinking that all knowledge hangs together in a unified structure. This makes the mistake of thinking that all the objects of knowledge together make up a single system, and can be known as such. But, Aristotle thinks, there is no such single system; different branches of knowledge employ fundamentally different methods, and do so because their subject-matters are fundamentally different. Aristotle does not disagree that something like Euclid's geometry is a reasonable model for knowledge; like Plato, he is willing to appeal to mathematics to beef up the idea of expertise. But there is no such thing as knowledge as a whole, only the different kinds or branches of knowledge – or, as we are tempted to say, sciences. (The Greek word for knowledge, *episteme*, forms a plural, but we cannot say 'knowledges', and have to make do either with 'branches of knowledge' or 'sciences'. This can obscure the way that, for example, Aristotle's notion of a science is a restriction of Plato's conception of knowledge.)

As well as this radical 'departmentalizing' of knowledge, Aristotle imports a further difference. Whereas Plato focuses relentlessly on the individual knower, Aristotle widens his epistemological view to take in many aspects of the *social* production of knowledge. It is not for nothing that 'science' is more appropriate to Aristotle's discussions of knowledge than to Plato's. Aristotle is aware of the way that the development of a science, such as biology, requires research and observation from many people, and also that the single investigator does not reinvent the wheel every time, but relies on others' results and data and, more importantly, on their questions and setting of the problems. He himself begins his enquiries in a number of fields by first canvassing views on it that are reputable and widely held, or put forward by philosophers or other investigators. It is by entering into this tradition of previous enquiry and exploring the problems that it has thrown up that the investigator can make progress.

Hence Aristotle can distinguish (though it would have been nice if he had done so more clearly) between different aspects of the development of a body of knowledge. The data and observations a science relies on, built up by the co-operative activities of many people, are material for a science, not science itself. Pieces of information do not constitute knowledge until they are fitted into and form part of a structured system. Hence before they amount to knowledge, the results of research and observation must be given a place within the appropriate structure. In the *Posterior Analytics* this structure is laid out very rigidly, and the influence of the mathematical model is very obvious. The first principles of a science must be true, primary and immediate, hold necessarily and be explanatory of the results that they are the first principles of. Much effort has gone into exploring ways in which a science like, say, biology could fit such a model, and it is generally agreed that the model is unsuitably rigid for many Aristotelian sciences. The overall point is not lost, however: empirical research is needed to gather any information worth knowing, but knowledge comes only when we see how it fits into a formal explanatory structure.

Both Plato and Aristotle have an extremely ideal model of understanding. Neither doubts that knowledge is possible in principle, though for Plato particularly the conditions become very idealized and removed from everyday life. Of course, given that they are working with the expertise model, the idea that knowledge is possible is not very radical. But what they are claiming is that we can have knowledge not merely of humdrum matters but of philosophically challenging and worthwhile subjects. Some version of this claim is common in most ancient philosophical schools.

Scepticism and belief

This is not the only approach to knowledge, however; we find very different ones. The most radical of these is traced in part to Socrates and in part to Pyrrho, a later philosopher who also wrote nothing. This is ancient scepticism (making Socrates one founder of scepticism). Unlike modern scepticism, the ancient movement does not limit itself to denying that knowledge is possible, leaving us with true belief. Ancient scepticism is as concerned with holding beliefs as with knowledge, and is best thought of as an intellectual position concerning the powers of reason, one far more radical than modern scepticisms.

The sceptic begins like everyone else, by searching for truth and for knowledge. This he does by investigating, querying others' reasons for what they claim, and looking for supporting reasons for positions of his own. So far there is no disagreement with the basic idea that knowledge requires the giving of a reasoned account. Knowledge of any kind worth having (that is, not knowledge of everyday bits of information) requires that you be able to give satisfactory reasons for what you claim. What distinguishes the sceptic from other philosophers is just that he never regards himself as having got to that point. The Greek term *skeptikos* means, not a negative doubter, but an investigator, someone going in for *skeptesthai* or enquiry. As the late sceptic author Sextus Empiricus puts it, there are dogmatic philosophers, who think that they have found the truth; negative dogmatists, who feel entitled to the position that the truth cannot be found; and the sceptics, who are unlike both the other groups in that they are not committed either way. They are still investigating things.

Why the problem? Surely if you investigate you will turn up *some* results that can count as knowledge or at least as belief. Sceptics think that, while we want to think this, it will always turn out to be rash (or 'precipitate') assent: we committed ourselves too soon. Real inquiry, thorough investigation, will reveal that the situation was more complex

Pyrrho of Elis (c.360–c.270 BC) is, like Socrates, an influential philosopher who inspired others but wrote nothing himself. His life is even more elusive than that of Socrates, and unlike him he left no visual image.

Originally a painter, Pyrrho at some point was influenced by various philosophical schools. He accompanied Alexander the Great on his conquest of northern India, where he encountered Indian 'gymnosophists' or naked wise men. It has been claimed that this encounter was decisive for his own philosophical stance, and similarities have been claimed between reports of his arguments and early northern Indian Buddhist texts. The Greeks, however, found no problem in interpreting Pyrrhonism in Greek terms, especially as Pyrrhonists always argue against the views of others, and so developed a repertory of attacks on existing philosophical theories.

Pyrrho himself impressed others by the example of tranquillity and impeturbability he gave in refusing to commit himself to any dogmatic belief. Stories about him abound, but are mostly hostile jokes to the effect that he suspended judgement in everyday matters, thereby making himself ridiculous. Other stories say that he lived a respectable life and that Elis exempted philosophers from taxation in his honour. His pupil Timon wrote satires against dogmatic philosophers, and also prose accounts of Pyrrho's arguments which, though problematic, show them as forerunners to the later versions of these arguments, especially those found in our main sceptical text, Sextus Empiricus' *Outlines of Pyrrhonism* (of uncertain date but probably second century AD).

and problematic; we turn out never to have reason to commit ourselves one way or the other, and so end up suspending judgement – that is, having a detached and uncommitted attitude to whatever the issue was.

At first this sounds ridiculous, indeed unserious. Does the sceptic really hold that we can never establish what time it is, that the sun is shining, that this is bread and not grass? This is an ancient reaction, but a mistaken one.

Pyrrho, the founding figure of one branch of scepticism, is someone about whom we know little, and our accounts of his intellectual attitudes are frustratingly meagre. His uncompromising attitude about our never having reason to commit ourselves to anything led to unfriendly jokes, such as that he had to be looked after by unsceptical friends to stop him walking off cliffs, and the like. But there is an alternative tradition to the effect that he lived a normal life, so it is most probable that, like later sceptics, he took it that even when we cannot commit ourselves to beliefs we can live by the way things appear to us.

Later sceptics who took their inspiration from Pyrrho developed the idea that we 'live by appearances'. That is, all we need to live is for things to appear to us in one way rather than another. If we go beyond this (which we get inclined to do when we move on from everyday matters to issues where there is dispute and complexity) and try to commit ourselves to beliefs, we will always in fact find, if we investigate rigorously, that we cannot commit ourselves; there turns out to be equally good reason on both sides of the question, so that we find ourselves equally inclined both ways, and so end up uncommitted, suspending judgement on the issue. This does not leave us paralyzed, however, since we still have the appearances to live by. The fact that I cannot commit myself does not stop things appearing to me one way rather than another. Being rationally uncommitted does not do away with all the other sources of motivation that get us by – habit, desire,

71

fear of the law and so on. The view that if reason does not commit us we cannot go on living comes from an over-estimation of the powers of reason, which we do not always need and which tempts the dogmatist into committing herself prematurely to the truth of some theory.

Moreover, the sceptics go on the offensive here. What we want out of rational commitment to our beliefs, they hold, is happiness, which is to be found in peace of mind; we want to feel confident about the way things are and not worried by our uncertainty about them. But commitment to positive or negative theories on the topic can never do this; all it can do is displace or redirect the original anxiety. Only the sceptic, who realizes the futility of commitment to belief, is tranquil; rigorous investigation brings suspension of belief, and this brings the peace of mind that had been sought in the wished-for answers. Hence only the sceptic gets what everyone else is looking for, peace of mind. But she gets it only by not looking for it, merely being there when it arrives; and it arrives as a result of the rigorous investigation that makes it impossible to commit yourself for or against any position.

There is much in the sceptical story that is implausible, or seems forced. Moreover, problems lurk which can be barely mentioned here. What is the scope of the sceptic's suspension of belief? Does it extend only to matters on which she investigates? If so, does she have some beliefs, namely the unproblematic ones? Anyway, what is the sceptic doing telling us all this about how to achieve peace of mind, how others fail, and the sceptic succeeds? How can she do this without holding beliefs?

Ancient scepticism is one of the most interesting and subtle philosophical positions. Like its dogmatic cousins, it embodies strong assumptions about reason, though subversive rather than positive ones, and is both deeper and broader than modern forms of scepticism which limit themselves to complaints about knowledge, and may reject some subject-matters on the basis of uncritically accepting others. Ancient sceptics, unlike moderns, are uninterested in carving out a position within philosophy; they think that philosophical reason, when exercised, will always undermine itself.

Socrates provided an alternative inspiration for the other branch of ancient scepticism, which took over Plato's Academy from the middle of the third century BC until its end in the first century BC. The Academics held that philosophizing in the spirit of Plato should take the form of doing what Socrates did, namely undermining the claims of others while putting forward none of your own. Hence the sceptical Academics spent their time arguing *ad hominem* (that is, not from any position of their own but only from premises the opponent accepts) against dogmatic philosophers whose claims they thought inadequately grounded, mostly the Stoics. Unlike the Pyrrhonists, the Academics made no claims about happiness or peace of mind. Their assumption about reason is simply that dogmatic philosophers have always been too hasty; their claims can be overturned from within and not by relying on the establishment of other positions.

Varieties of knowledge

So far we have seen bold and radical positions, both positive and negative, about knowledge and belief. It would be misleading, however, to give the impression that ancient concerns with knowledge always focus on wisdom and understanding; we can also find concerns which overlap with modern ones. Plato, for example, produces interesting arguments against relativist theories of knowledge which do not rely on any of the special features of his own ambitious account. A relativist, such as Protagoras, against whom Plato argues in the dialogue *Theaetetus*, claims that for someone to have a true belief is no more than for something to appear true to him, and hence that truth is relative to the believer. This can seem at first like a liberating discovery, especially since it defuses all disagreement. The wind appears hot to me, cold to you; we are both right, and there is nothing to argue about. Protagoras, however, puts his relativist theory forward as a *theory*, something we should accept and take seriously (if only in order to be liberated from our disagreements). But if Protagoras is right, the truth of his own theory is relative to him – that is, it is just the way things appear to him. And why ever should we accept, or be interested in, what happens to appear a certain way to Protagoras? If we are to take relativism seriously as a theory, then relativism cannot hold of it. (Versions of this powerful point are still being made against modern forms of relativism.)

Plato is also interested in the question of what is going on when we are said to know particular facts, and this is developed by the Stoics, who retain the expertise model for what they call knowledge proper, but also develop an account of what they call apprehension, which amounts to one way of thinking of knowledge, especially in some modern epistemological theories. Apprehension is what you have when you are so related to an empirical fact that you cannot be wrong about it. The Stoics put some effort into working out what the conditions have to be for this to hold. Roughly, the thing in question has to make an impact on you, an impression; and this impression must come from the thing in the right way – the causal story must be the right one; and the impression must be one that you could not have had from any *other* thing, however similar. These conditions were seen as a challenge to produce counter-examples, where the conditions are all met, but we have to agree that we do not have knowledge. The Academic Sceptics in particular carried on a long debate with the Stoics on this topic, as a result of which the Stoics seem to have introduced further conditions and modifications.

Finally, we do find, in the range of ancient epistemological theories, one which seems to meet the desiderata for a modern theory, namely that of Epicurus. For Epicurus does worry about scepticism in the modern sense – that is, the person who rejects the idea that our beliefs might ever meet the criteria for knowledge – and he thinks that he has to establish the possibility of knowledge against this challenge. He thinks of knowledge not in terms of the expertise model, but in terms of the knower's relation to particular matters of fact. What I know, then, are for Epicurus primarily particular pieces of information to which I am related in such a way that my relation to them constitutes knowledge; these are the primary items that are known. Anything more ambitious than this has to be shown to be built out from these primary items in the most economical and careful way that is feasible.

Epicurus' theory is, untypically for ancient theories, rigorously empiricist – that is, it begins from and relies on our sense-experience. What I know comes to me through the senses, since only sensations relate information to me in a way which is unmediated by a process which could involve error. My ordinary beliefs, arrived at in ways which involve inferences going beyond experience, contain truths, but also falsehoods that have crept in through the human propensity to get things wrong. But if I concentrate only on what the senses tell me, I cannot go wrong. For Epicurus, belief and reasoning are sources of error, not, as for most other schools, the source of our ability to correct error. Error, then, comes in only when I start adding beliefs to what the senses tell me. Hence it turns out that what the senses tell me is not even as extensive as claims about tables and towers – since obviously these can be mistaken, as when we judge from a distance that a square tower is round. Rather, the reports of the senses are limited to how the tower appears to us from a particular perspective at a particular place, and so on. Hence we have knowledge, since we cannot be wrong about this. We could, however, be wrong about the tower, since we might make a claim that did not make due allowance for perspective, distance etc. Our knowledge turns out to be far more limited than our everyday observations about the world around us.

Epicurus' theory of knowledge was not regarded as particularly impressive; indeed it was widely regarded as hideously crude. Later Epicureans, however, did develop interesting analogues of what we think of as issues of induction – how, from a number of particular observations, we can come to make justifiable generalizations about *all* occurrences of this kind of thing. Are we justified, for example ('we' being Epicurean philosophers living in Italy) in inferring that because all the humans we have observed are mortal, so are humans in hitherto undiscovered countries, such as Britain? (If there are any humans there, adds Philodemus, the philosopher whose example this is.)

Empiricist theories of knowledge, like an emphasis on the knower's relation to particular facts, are the minority stream in ancient epistemology. What emerges from even a cursory survey of ancient concerns with knowledge, however, is the width and diversity of approaches. A student of epistemology in the ancient world would find a number of challenging theories and an extensive tradition of debate. She would find several ways of understanding *knowledge*: theories about wisdom and theories about apprehension of particular facts, theories privileging abstract reasoning and theories privileging the basic reports of the senses. She would also find extensive engagement not just with knowledge, but more generally with problems of belief and the powers of reasoning, both positive and negative.

Chapter 5
Logic and reality

The syllabus

If you specialize in philosophy at university, you discover that there are
some skills you have to acquire, and topics you have to cover, in order to
become competent in the subject. You will have to do some courses in
logic and critical thinking, and cover topics in metaphysics,
epistemology (and possibly philosophy of science), and in ethics,
political philosophy (and possibly aesthetics). You may also have to do
some history of philosophy, which will almost certainly be done in a way
critical of philosophers, past and present, in what are seen as 'other'
traditions, although philosophers in what is seen as 'your' tradition will
be treated more respectfully.

In the ancient world things were not so different. After the
establishment of Plato's Academy, philosophical schools devoted to
different philosophical traditions were the major places where
philosophy was learnt, taught and passed on. Wealthy individuals might
have philosophy tutors in their homes, but these would typically have
been trained in some philosophical school. Each school would belong to
a definite tradition, within which certain texts (typically Aristotle's, or
the Stoics') were privileged. And from fairly early on the philosophical
curriculum consisted of three parts: logic, physics and ethics. This
happened early enough for it to be ascribed (unconvincingly) to Plato,

though it is clear that neither Plato nor Aristotle wrote with such a curriculum in mind; it fits the interests of later schools, like the Stoics and Epicureans, far better. So far we have looked at an important topic in the ethics part of the curriculum, and also at theory of knowledge, which was considered part of logic, since logic was construed broadly, so as to cover what we call epistemology and philosophy of language. But there was also logic as we generally understand the term, more narrowly. And there is the topic that sounds oddest to us, 'physics'.

Logic

Why is logic needed as part of philosophy? This topic was controversial then as now, some holding that logic was a part of philosophy in its own right, others that it was only a 'tool' that we use in order to improve our study of philosophy proper. Either way, we need logic to ensure that our arguments are sound ones, with no lurking fallacies for opponents to exploit, and also to enable us to detect weaknesses in the ways our opponents argue. In ancient philosophy logic has the function of sustaining philosophical truths and demolishing philosophical mistakes. Logic developed for its own sake was often regarded as a potential distraction from the central concerns of philosophy.

Logic is one of the more impressive achievements of Aristotle. Finding no given systematic techniques for classifying and distinguishing arguments that just persuade people from arguments which lead to true conclusions by valid inferences (and also finding, as today, many influential people glorying in conflating the two), Aristotle systematized the notion of valid argument and constructed an extensive logical system.

The centre of Aristotle's logic is the idea of a *deduction*, in Greek *sullogismos*. He defines it quite generally: a deduction is an argument in which, some things having been laid down, something other than the things laid down comes about by necessity, because these things are so.

More formally, the conclusion of a deduction follows necessarily from the premises. Aristotle adds that the conclusion must be something *different* from the premises; hence he is not trying to capture what modern logicians are after when they hold that 'If p then p' is a valid argument. He also holds that the truth of the conclusion must come about in a way that is *through* the truth of the premises, thus excluding redundant premises making no contribution in establishing the truth of the conclusion. Here too he diverges from modern notions of purely formal inference. There has been a large amount of (unsettled) modern discussion as to what Aristotelian deductions are, in terms of modern formal logic, and hence as to how his logic should be classified.

In modern terms Aristotle's is only a fragment of logic, since, despite the wide scope of his definition of a deduction, he systematically studies only a much narrower range of deductions, those that have come to be known as Aristotelian syllogisms. He considers statements, positive and negative, that have the form of claiming that a predicate *P*, 'belongs to' or does not 'belong to' a subject *S*, in all, some or no cases. (As developed since the Middle Ages, these statements take the more familiar form of 'All *S*s are *P*', 'Some *S*s are *P*', 'Some *S*s are not *P*', and 'No *S*s are *P*'.) Aristotle's greatest contribution is the use of schematic letters, which enables him to study the form of an argument regardless of its particular content. He systematizes the ways in which two statements in one of these forms, which share a common term (the 'middle' term) lead to a conclusion. Some of these combinations will give valid arguments, others not. Aristotle devotes great ingenuity to showing which forms are valid, and which are not. (He also begins to develop a system of 'modal logic', that is, a logic of statements modified by 'necessarily', 'possibly' and so on, but less successfully.)

Various suggestions have been made as to why Aristotle should have limited himself in this way. Fairly plausible is the idea that, although he is interested in arguments as such, Aristotle is most concerned to formalize the type of argument which finds its home in his model of a completed science or body of knowledge, one in which what is at stake is the relations of kinds of thing, and claims about what holds universally are particularly important. Arguments involving individuals find no place in this logical system (though they appear in fleeting thoughts on Aristotle's part about a 'practical' logic of arguments that lead to action).

Aristotle hints at ideas, developed further by his pupil Theophrastus, of systematizing arguments where what is studied are the relations between the statements, rather than the terms which form part of them. Real progress here, however, was left to the Stoics, in particular Chrysippus. Stoic logic concerns statements or *axiomata*, which assert or deny something. Compound statements are produced by joining simple statements by various connectives, such as 'and', 'or' and 'if'. Stoic logic studies arguments which are made up of premises and conclusion, where these are all statements; much of it overlaps with modern 'propositional logic', though there are differences. Five argument-schemata are taken as basic (the schematic letters P and Q stand in for statements). These are: (1) If P, then Q, P; therefore, Q (still familiar, as 'modus ponens'), (2) If P, then Q, not-Q; therefore not-P ('modus tollens'), (3) Not both P and Q, P; therefore not-Q, (4) Either P or Q, P; therefore, not-Q, (5) Either P or Q, not-P, therefore Q. From this basis Stoic logic developed in sophisticated and powerful ways.

As with Aristotle, the Stoics were not merely interested in argument for its own sake. They were concerned to produce arguments which were also 'proofs' – arguments which, as they put it, 'by way of agreed premises, reveal by deduction an unclear conclusion'. Logical form is studied in the service of representing our claims to knowledge, in this case the way we claim to reach knowledge of 'unclear' or theoretical matters by way of what we can agree on in our experience.

Epicurus and his school affected to despise formal logic as a trivial waste of time. But they also spent energy on studying what were called 'signs' on the basis of which we make inferences from what we experience to matters that are beyond our own experience; so they engaged other schools in discussion about logic to some extent.

Students of philosophy in the ancient world could (unless they were Epicureans) expect to study both Aristotelian and Stoic logic, which were seen as complementary, although there could be disputes as to which was the more important. By historical accident, Stoic logic was lost, along with much early Stoicism, at the end of antiquity, whereas Aristotle's logic not only survived but became regarded as all there was to logic. It was elaborated in the Middle Ages, regarded as complete by Kant and dislodged from its place in the syllabus only by the rediscovery of propositional logic by Frege and Russell at the beginning of the twentieth century.

Nature and science

The third part of the philosophical curriculum, 'physics', no longer sounds as though it even belongs to philosophy. This is partly because of our narrowing of a term which originally meant the study of *nature* or *phusis*. Nature is just everything that there is, or the world (including humans, who are part of the world). Hence the study of nature can cover a number of very different things, and 'physics' covers a range of enquiries which for us have got segregated into different subject-matters and taught in very different ways.

One type of enquiry seeks explanations for the puzzling things we see around us and are exposed to. What explains the regularities of the sun and the moon? What brings about the seasons, so crucial for farmers? Why are there hurricanes, earthquakes, eclipses? In the ancient world these were regarded as issues which were part of the study of nature as philosophers undertook that. As philosophy developed, however, and especially after Aristotle, these questions lost much of their interest, since there were numbers of theories about them, but no decisive ways of deciding between these, and so no convincing way of showing any given answer to be correct. They became regarded as suitable material for dinner-party discussion rather than live philosophical questions. In the modern world, of course, the advances of science, whatever their other drawbacks, have provided us with firm answers to questions like these. They no longer seem remotely philosophical, and ancient discussions of them are often put into the history of science.

The study of nature narrowed in another way also, especially in the period after Aristotle, with the development of bodies of scientific knowledge separate from philosophy. Medicine, though crude by modern standards, developed as a specialized science, with differing schools. It was the mathematical sciences, however, which made the greatest strides, with Euclid's *Elements* a high point. Archimedes was not only a great mathematician, but developed astronomy and also applied branches like engineering. Historians of science sometimes lament the fact that sophisticated technical ideas were applied in trivial ways; Heron of Alexandria describes a machine for making figures mechanically pour libations on an altar. But basic facts about the ancient economies precluded anything like the development of our industrial technology. Whether we are obviously the winners here is another matter.

Physics and metaphysics

The study of nature, or 'physics' in the ancient sense, however, covered more than what became narrow scientific enquiries. From the beginning, 'nature' could be used for 'what there is', everything that there is to be studied. Hence much of ancient 'physics' is so broad as to correspond to what we think of as metaphysics. Is change a necessary feature of our world? What is change, anyway? In the world around us, what are the real entities, the things that are basic to a true view of the way the world *really* is? Are living things, like animals and humans, such basic entities? They seem to be the subjects of changes, the things changes happen to. But if what is real is the subject of change, then perhaps in looking for what is real we should not stop with the living things, but look for whatever it is which in them is the subject of change. Perhaps this is the material they are made out of. Issues like this are central to the philosophical enquiries of many of the so-called Presocratics and of Aristotle, who engaged with their ideas and is our major source for many of them. They are not part of modern science, but of more abstract philosophical enquiries, generally called metaphysical. Often the dividing-line between Aristotle's 'physics' and his 'metaphysics' is a thin one.

Such questions were thought to arise naturally in the context of a general view of the world as a whole. Given the less ambitious scope of modern metaphysics, they are often studied in relative isolation. Thus we tend to see Plato's 'theory of Forms', for example, as a metaphysical theory that has nothing to do with what we think of as physics or the study of nature. In the ancient world, however, it was mostly seen as one aspect of Plato's 'physics' or theory of the world, which was primarily studied in the *Timaeus*, a dialogue not very popular today which contains Plato's cosmology or account of the universe and its structure.

Plato's 'theory of Forms'

Plato has no explicit theory of Forms. In some dialogues, especially *Phaedo*, *Republic*, *Symposium*, *Phaedrus*, and *Timaeus*, there are passages, some with argument and others more expressive and metaphorical, which introduce in various ways items we usually call Forms, but for which Plato never develops a standard terminology.

In contrast to the things in our experience which are beautiful,

Plato introduces the idea of the 'beautiful itself', which is beautiful in a way not relative to context or time or perspective. Unlike all the beautiful things and people in our experience, the beautiful itself is never not beautiful. This idea is developed with value terms like *beautiful*, *just*, and *good*, and with mathematical terms like *double* and *half*. It is notoriously unclear how Plato's arguments could be extended beyond terms with opposites. Despite a widely misinterpreted passage in the *Republic*, Plato does not think that there is a Form for every general term; Forms are not what came to be called universals. There is a Form only where there is an objective nature that can be known by being intellectually grasped; Forms are always associated with using your mind to reason, as opposed to relying uncritically on your sense experience. The most famous passages about Forms stress this contrast between the mindless assumption that what experience impresses on you is just what there is, and the critical use of reason to grasp realities, the Forms, that are accessible only to the enquiring mind.

In the dialogue *Parmenides* Plato shows that he is aware of apparent inconsistencies in what he has said about Forms. The right response, however, he holds, is not to abandon Forms but to continue to argue on both sides until a defensible position is reached. He continued in this spirit, never successfully producing a definitive theory of Forms. Later philosophers have often simplified the issues, but Aristotle and late twentieth century philosophers have explored the different arguments Plato employs for and against the existence of Forms.

What you studied as 'physics' or metaphysics in the ancient world would depend a great deal on what tradition of philosophy you primarily belonged to. Epicureans, for example, held that physical and metaphysical questions mattered only to the extent that getting the answers to them wrong led us to be disturbed and unhappy; getting interested in them for their own sake was a misuse of time that would be better employed learning more directly how to live well. The Stoics thought it important to get right the major metaphysical points about the world: it is governed by providence, and a rational appreciation of it will discern how everything in it is for the best. But they were not much more interested than the Epicureans in getting the details right for their own sake.

Aristotle on nature

Among ancient philosophies it is the Aristotelian tradition which has the broadest and most generous conception of what the study of nature is. Aristotle had the reputation of being the philosopher most interested in causes and explanations. And, although his account of nature is not one that we, with our modern scientific knowledge, can still accept, we can still appreciate the main lines of it as embodying a response to our world which is highly worthy of respect.

For Aristotle, nature is the world made up of things that have natures. What is it to have a nature? It is to be a thing which has a source internal to itself of changing and being changed. We can understand what a lion is only by looking at lions themselves and at the way they interact with their environment and other species. To understand an artefact like a shield, by contrast, we have to appeal to something external to the shield itself – the designs of humans that made it. Things with natures are primarily living things, such as plants and animals, including humans. For Aristotle, then, nature is, right from the start, not just whatever happens, the undifferentiated totality of what there is (as it is for Mill and others from the nineteenth century on). Nature is already a world of things that organize themselves and live characteristic lives, and to understand nature is to come to understand what kind of lives these are. Nature is active, a system of living and changing things. There is no hint in Aristotle of the view, notorious in many scientists since the early modern period, that nature is passive, lying out there to be mastered by the scientific mind.

Still less is there the even more notorious idea that nature is there for us to exploit. For Aristotle, skill and expertise take further what nature has begun. He is thinking of farmers who breed grasses to produce food crops, and of cooking as a process of predigestion to enable us to consume otherwise inedible foods. It never occurs to him to think of technology as invasive of nature. (Doubtless this is partly because he is not aware of any technology sophisticated enough to do this.) Nor does it occur to him that human activities might upset nature's established balances. Humans hunt and eat animals and fish in the way these hunt one another and eat plants; it is all part of a self-regulating system. Many of Aristotle's ideas are, tragically, bound to sound quaint in our world, where humans have intervened disastrously in the workings of nature, wrecking ecosystems and exterminating species. For Aristotle the species, including humans, have always been there and always will be; what we want is to understand how they all fit in overall. That is why, in a famous passage, he defends the study of the 'lower' animals and how they work as being as worthy a human study as the grander study of the heavenly bodies. 'For in all natural things there is something wonderful.'

For Aristotle, we want to understand nature, including ourselves as parts of nature, because it is natural for humans to want to understand things. Isn't this circular, though? Yes, but the circularity does not matter. Aristotle's theories are naturalistic in the modern sense; they accept that the processes by which we come to understand nature are themselves a part of nature. They are not something mysteriously exempt from the conditions they study. Philosophy, including the study of nature, begins in wonder; we are puzzled and interested by what we find around us, and do not feel satisfied until we have adequate explanations for it. The search for explanation thus does not point beyond itself; for Aristotle it would be beside the point, as well as

Aristotle's 'four causes'

Aristotle insists, against what he sees as the narrowness of previous philosophers, that there are four 'causes' which the enquirer into nature should make use of. What he has in mind is the different ways in which we explain natural processes and things, and he is insisting that there is not just one type of explanation, but many, which do not exclude one another. Aristotle's theory, though, is about the way the world is and not just the way we explain it; the four so-called 'causes' are different kinds of item which figure in what he thinks are the four fundamental types of explanation of nature.

One is the material cause or matter, the physical make-up of the thing, which puts considerable restrictions on what it can be and do. The second is the form. Aristotle gives examples of artefacts where the form is the shape, but in the case of a living thing the form is more complex: it is, very roughly, the way of being alive which defines that kind of thing. The form of an oak tree is whatever it is which explains why the tree lives and grows *as an oak* – from acorns, for example, and only in certain climates. Thirdly is the moving cause, the item initiating a change. Fourthly is the final cause or end, what the thing or process is for, something that has to be cited in showing how it functions.

Modern theories of causality have very different aims and assumptions, and would count only Aristotle's moving cause as a cause (and only with qualifications).

foolish, for us to try to understand nature in order to exploit it for our own ends. Hence, although different methods are appropriate for studying different areas of nature, we are puzzled, and seek explanations, in our own case in the same way as happens with other living and non-living things.

Explaining is finding out *why* things are as they are, and for Aristotle there are four basic ways of doing this, his so-called 'four causes', which appeal to what he calls form, matter, the moving cause, and the final cause, what the thing is for.

Teleology without design

Aristotle is aware that his demand for teleological explanations, explanations in terms of final causes or what something is for, is contentious. He knows of previous thinkers who held that there are no goals in nature, and that we and the world around us are the contingent products of random events. Animals' teeth, for example, were held by some to be the product of random combinations of material, some of which turned out to be suited to animals' needs while others were not.

Aristotle, as often, does not think that this story is *completely* wrong; we do need the right kind of physical embodiment. But on its own it is inadequate to explain why we *always* (or nearly always) find that animals are well adapted to the lives they lead, and that their parts are formed in a way which performs the appropriate function. Teeth, for example: we find the sharp incisors at the front of the mouth, for tearing, and the blunt molars at the back, for chewing. We always find this, because it is a good arrangement for the animal. Unless something has gone wrong, we don't find animals struggling with bad arrangements (molars at the front, for example). Random happenings, Aristotle thinks, are quite inadequate as an explanation of how we get to the universal well-adaptedness to environments and lifestyles that we find among animals. Thus, he concludes, our explanations have to include what the thing is for. Aristotle does not think that this is always appropriate: there is nothing, for example, that horses or camels are for. The level of explanation that concerns him is that of the parts of animals. Hearts, for example, are for pumping out the blood to the rest of the body; blood, in turn, is for carrying nutriment to the body.

Aristotle's is an especially interesting position, because we can now appreciate both that he is wrong, and that at the time he had the better of the argument. In the absence of any plausible mechanism for getting to (almost) universal well-adaptedness from random happenings, as well as the absence of any idea of geological time, Aristotle is right in thinking that present well-adaptedness cannot be accounted for merely by random happenings. After Darwin's work, we can see why we are not compelled to an Aristotelian view by the kind of consideration that Aristotle stresses.

Aristotle's teleological approach is the source of his most sympathetic insights. In plants, he comments, the roots have the function that the head has in animals; but we should not think of plants as growing upside down, since what is up and what down depends on the kind of thing we are talking about. Crabs are the only animals which move sideways; but in a sense they are moving forwards, since their eyes are so positioned that they can see where they are going. In these and many other cases Aristotle frees himself from human ways of thinking of things like nutrition and movement to observe how well the species functions from its own point of view.

Aristotle's thoughts about teleology have nothing to do with the idea that purposes in nature are the product of design – indeed, for him this would be inappropriate projection of human concerns onto nature, shaping nature in our image in an absurdly pretentious way. But Aristotle's was not the only version of teleology available in the ancient world.

Teleology with design

In his dialogue *Timaeus*, Plato presents an account of the universe as created by God, who is a craftsman and who produces our universe in the way that a craft worker creates an artefact, by imposing form and order on materials which are more or less satisfactory for the task. Plato holds that the materials available to God for making the world are inherently unsatisfactory and perhaps even refractory, since our world is created to a good plan, but contains failure and evil.

It is uncertain, and was much discussed in the ancient world, whether Plato had in mind an actual creation or was merely giving an analysis of the ways things are, but certainly the overall picture is one in which our world is not just created, but created to carry out an intellectual design on the part of a creator. Moreover, not merely the general principles of cosmology, but some quite specific details, particularly concerning humans, are explained in terms of overall design. The fact that humans walk upright, and have roughly spherical heads, is explained by reference to our being rational in a way that other animals are not; the explanations, as we might expect, are extremely fanciful.

The *Timaeus*, however, presents itself not as serious cosmology but merely as a 'likely story', an example of the kind of account that Plato thinks is the right one to give; it is poetic and grandiose in style. And the account it gives is also very openly 'top-down', working through the consequences of a few very general principles; Plato shows no interest in satisfying the observations we make in our experience, or in making any himself.

The Stoics picked up on Plato's account of the world as the creation of a designer God, and developed it, though in a somewhat different direction. Their conception of God is different; for them God is to be thought of not as a creator of the world, but in a more impersonal way. God is simply the rational organization of the world, and so should not be thought of on the model of a person (though the Stoics allow that popular religion, which accepts several gods, is a dim grasp of the idea that the world is structured by reason and intelligence).

The Stoics therefore take a different tack from Plato's appeal to the idea that God is like a craftsman. They appeal to evidence in the world that suggests that it is the product of design and rational ordering. They reject the idea that the world is the product of random events and forces, on the grounds that it is implausible – like, they say, the idea that random distribution of letters of the alphabet could produce a poem. (Note that this argument is different from Aristotle's; he denies that random events could produce regular well-adaptedness, whereas the Stoics deny that random events could produce good design.)

Some of their arguments for design in the world appeal to the sheer complexity of natural objects. Suppose, one argument goes, that a complicated mechanism like a clock were shown to people unfamiliar with it; they would still recognize it as the product of a rational being. Hence, natural objects, which display a greater complexity and suitability for their function than artefacts, must be the product of reason – clearly a reason greater than ours, one embodied in the universe as a whole. (This is strikingly similar to the 'argument from design' common among Christian thinkers before Darwin.)

Other arguments appeal to the complexity of the world's organization, seen as a huge ecosystem in which all the parts are mutually interdependent. The Stoics also appeal to the way that animals are well-suited to their environments and mutual interrelations, but they are not interested in these for their own sakes, merely for the indication they give that the world is a well-organized whole.

Thinking of the world as designed, the Stoics often compare it to a house or a city, and since these are obviously designed for the sake of their inhabitants, this makes prominent the point that for the Stoics the world is rationally designed for the obvious beneficiaries, namely rational beings – that is, gods and humans. As far as humans are concerned, therefore, the rest of the world – plants and animals – is designed for our benefit. This leads the Stoics to a very anthropocentric view of the world, in which grain, olives and vines are for us to consume, sheep for clothing us with their fleeces, oxen for pulling our ploughs and so forth. Such a world-view is almost guaranteed to kill the curiosity about nature's wonders that we find in Aristotle, and it leads to an exploitative attitude to the rest of the natural world, a strikingly ugly contrast to the humanitarian attitude we find in Stoic thought to all humans, whatever their social roles.

No teleology?

Epicurus alone among the ancient schools denies that in nature we find any teleological explanations. Nothing in nature is *for* anything, neither the world as a whole nor anything in it.

Positively, Epicurus asserts that our world, and in the course of time infinitely many worlds, have grown up as a result of random collisions of atoms in empty space. This is, he claims, a sufficient explanation, given enough time. We have seen that given the state of other beliefs about the world in ancient culture (for example the absence of any indication of the real age of the world), Epicurus' position here was bound to seem weaker than it does to us, and one reason that one or other form of teleology was so common in ancient thought was just the implausibility of the alternative.

Epicurus also argues against the opposition, and here appeals to the idea that an unbiased view of our world does not make it look like the product of design, or at any rate of a very good design. Most of the world is not habitable by humans, for example; human attempts to survive are constantly threatened by the unpredictability of natural factors (droughts, hurricanes and so on) and by hostile environments and other species that render human life a struggle. Humans, with their helpless babyhood and lack of natural weapons, do not seem particularly well-adapted to compete for survival with other species. And so on.

Epicurus' arguments are effective only against the view that the world was providentially designed for the benefit of humans. Even so, there are responses: perhaps the problems humans encounter are due to the fact that rational design in the universe has only inferior materials to order. And Epicurus never really meets the point that with no appeal to any kind of purpose in nature he has a hard time explaining how random collisions of atoms result in the *regular* well-adaptedness of species to their environments.

Ancient theories and the modern world

The legacy of these ancient disputes became greatly simplified. Already in the ancient world both Jews and Christians found Plato's *Timaeus* acceptable as a philosophical explication of the creation story in *Genesis*. This is not surprising, since the Judaeo-Christian God is the creator of the world, and designed it so as to be good. Moreover, humans have a privileged place in it. In the Middle Ages the view that prevailed was the design view: everything in the world, including us (indeed especially us) was created to fulfil its place in the world, which is to be found in God's design for it. Humans are the special beneficiaries of this plan, and the rest of creation is designed for us to put to our use.

In the Middle Ages, when Aristotle's views were rediscovered, they were fitted into the design view, since they were fitted into a theological framework in which the world is the creation of a designer God. Aristotle's own more subtle position was not appreciated; the only alternatives were seen as being that the world is the result of divine design or that it is the product of mere random happenings. The latter view was not taken seriously until the Renaissance, when Epicurus' views again became influential and inspired some philosophers to reject the entire medieval world-view.

This world-view included, and indeed had itself largely come to be formed by, the philosophy of Aristotle. But that itself had become greatly altered in the process. Aristotle's view of nature, including his ideas about ends in nature, had become part of a large theological system. In the process, his own tentative and co-operative methodology was forgotten as his ideas were hardened into a system, increasingly seen as a complete and all-inclusive system, with answers to everything. The medieval poet Dante calls Aristotle 'the master of those who know' – in other words, the great know-it-all, something very different in spirit from Aristotle's own enquiry in a spirit of curiosity and wonder.

The new learning of the Renaissance replaced the system of Aristotelianism, but because this had become deeply entrenched in the universities it hung on for surprisingly long, and became associated with self-protective and reactionary rejection of new kinds of thinking. A similar phenomenon happened with Aristotle's ethical and political thought, which was elevated to a central place by the Roman Catholic Church. This rigidification of Aristotle's thinking has led to equally unsubtle rejections of his ideas, and to refusal to engage with them in detail. In periods when Aristotle was regarded as The Great Authority, intelligent thinkers have often rejected that authority, while Aristotle's own attitude has been lost. Because Aristotle's own works are quite difficult to read, hostile attitudes to his ideas get passed on from book to book, and get accepted by people who have never actually engaged with him as a philosopher. Even today, it is quite common to find sometimes paranoid hostility to Aristotle on the part of people who have never read more than a few quotations pulled out of context and who think of him simply as an authority to be rejected.

This is an extreme example of the way in which ideas from ancient

Aristotle and authority

'The investigation of the truth is in one way hard, in another easy. An indication of this is found in the fact that no one is able to attain the truth adequately, while, on the other hand, no one fails entirely, but every one says something true about the nature of things, and while individually they contribute little or nothing to the truth, by the union of all a considerable amount is amassed. Therefore, since the truth seems to be like the pro-verbial barn door, which no one can fail to hit, in this way it is easy, but the fact that we can have a whole truth and not the particular part we aim at shows the difficulty of it . . . It is just that we should be grateful, not only to those whose opinions we may share, but also to those who have expressed more superficial views; for these also contributed something, by developing before us the powers of thought.'

Aristotle, *Metaphysics*, Book 2, Chapter 1

'When a Schoolman tells me *Aristotle hath said it*, all I conceive he means by it, is to dispose me to embrace his opinion with the deference and submission which custom has annexed to that name. And this effect may be so instantly produced in the minds of those who are accustomed to resign their judgement to the authority of that philosopher, as it is impossible any idea either of his person, writings or reputation should go before. So close and immediate a connexion may custom establish, betwixt the very word *Aristotle* and the motions of assent and reverence in the minds of some men.'

Bishop George Berkeley

philosophy can get used and reconfigured by subsequent traditions, in a way which pulls them out of their original context of argument. Sometimes this can be invigorating, and produce a new and fruitful

6. Aristotle, portrayed as serious and studious

engagement, as happened when Plato's *Republic* became a political text in the nineteenth century (see Chapter 2) and with Aristotle for much of the Middle Ages. But if the interpretative tradition goes on too long (especially without serious competition) and gets too rigid and institutionalized, the result can become stultifying, and can end with hostile unthinking rejection. And this makes it harder to get back to the original and engage with it from our own perspective.

Chapter 6
When did it all begin?
(and what is it anyway?)

Many people have turned expectantly to the beginnings of Greek
philosophy, only to find that the first philosopher they meet, Thales in
the sixth century BC, held, apparently, that 'everything is water'. Anyone
teaching ancient philosophy has to cope with the bafflement that this
discovery tends to produce. It is an odd beginning to a philosophical
tradition. Yet *something* happens in the sixth century, later to acquire
the name *philosophia* or love of wisdom, which we can recognize as
philosophical. What exactly is it?

It is in keeping with what we have seen of the varied and disputatious
nature of ancient philosophy that this question is quite hard to answer.
There is little that non-trivially unites philosophers from Thales to the
end of antiquity. There is a tradition, but a mixed and contested one.

In view of the great cultural prestige of Greek philosophy, it has at times
been resented, and sometimes groups that have felt themselves
culturally marginalized by it have claimed that Greek philosophy is
nothing new at all, but just a tradition taken over without
acknowledgement – usually, it is claimed, from the group in question.
The early Church fathers held that the pagan philosophers stole their
ideas from the Jewish scriptures. Afrocentric writers in the twentieth
century have made the same claim for Egyptian mystery religion. These
claims, however, are historically non-starters.

Differing views on the Greeks' originality

'What provokes admiration is the mental vigour and independence with which these people sought after coherent systems and did not shrink from following their lines of thought to astonishing conclusions. It may well be that contact with oriental cosmology and theology helped to liberate their imagination; it certainly gave them many suggestive ideas. But they taught themselves to reason. Philosophy as we understand it is a Greek idea.'

Martin West, 1986

'What is Plato but Moses writing in Greek?'

Numenius of Apamea (second century AD).

'We should not be surprised to say that the Greeks are capable of filching the beliefs of the Jews, given that they have not only plundered their other sciences from the Egyptians and Chaldaeans and other foreign nations, but even now can be caught robbing one another of their literary reputations . . .

'It is reasonable to think that the Greeks, who contributed nothing of their own in wisdom (only verbal facility and fluency) and filched everything from foreigners, should also have been aware of the sayings of the Jews and laid hands on these in turn . . . Not just my words but their own establish them as thieves . . .'

Eusebius, bishop of Caesarea (AD c.260–339)

The Greeks themselves did not think that philosophy was original with them; they thought of it as coming from a variety of sources outside Greece, usually Eastern. But then, they did not value originality as such very highly, and they certainly did think that philosophy was something that they did distinctively and well. And indeed, when we read the fragments even of an author as elusive as Thales we can see an interesting and distinctive way of thinking emerging.

A tradition of reasoning?

What makes it philosophical? Usually this is characterized as explicit appeal to *reason* and *argument*. Stated as generally as this, the claim is undoubtedly true. Philosophers are distinguished by arguing for their conclusions and against other philosophers' conclusions, and by demanding reasons for others' claims and giving reasons for their own. But while this may mark philosophy off from poetry and the like, it does not give us a very determinate way of proceeding, or of marking philosophy off from other intellectual endeavours. There are many kinds of reason and argument – which is to count? When we look at the different kinds of project that the Presocratics produced, we are hard put to find a single kind of reasoning at work, or a demand for a single kind of argument.

The first Presocratics, Thales, Anaximander, and Anaximenes – from Miletus in Asia Minor – were concerned to provide cosmologies, reasoned accounts of the world we live in. As Aristotle acutely saw, they focused on what he called the material cause – the question of what our world is composed of. This is the question to which we find answers in terms of water, air and 'the boundless'. These answers show a very striking degree of simplicity and economy, and bring with them explanations of a wide variety of puzzling physical phenomena. Because of this, these philosophers have at times been seen as precursors of science, with its explanatory hypotheses. It is clear, however, that there is little in these very speculative theories that can be usefully compared with any precise concept of scientific enquiry. A just account has to see these Presocratic figures as transitional, with an intellectual impulse to render our world

7. A late representation of Anaximander with a sundial he is credited with inventing

explicable which has much in common with later philosophy and science.

Other Presocratics are anything but scientific. Heraclitus of Ephesus writes in aphorisms of notorious obscurity, uniting an account of the world as fire with concern for the individual's self-knowledge. His account of both appeals to reason (*logos*), both your individual reason and the big Reason in the universe that your reason should try to conform to; yet there is little reason or argument to convince us of this. Xenophanes of Colophon uses reason and argument to undermine naive

A new way of thinking?

'My aim has been to show that a new thing came into the world with the early Ionian teachers – the thing we call science . . . It is quite wrong to look for the origins of Ionian science in mytho-logical ideas of any kind . . . It is to these men we owe the conception of an exact science which should ultimately take in the whole world as its object.'

John Burnet, 1892

'I have tried to show how the philosopher retains his prophetic character. He relies for his vision of divinity and of the real nature of things on the assumed identity of his own reason with a portion of the cosmic consciousness . . . The intuitive reason replaces that supernormal faculty which had formerly been active in dreams and prophetic visions; the supernatural becomes the metaphysical . . . It would have been a miracle if the wise men of the sixth century . . . should have swept their minds clean of all mythical preconceptions.'

Francis Cornford, 1952

beliefs about the gods. In him we see clearly for the first time reason being used to fault and replace ordinary beliefs by something the philosopher argues to be more rationally adequate. Anthropomorphic views of God are shown to be defective in a convincing way: every people, Xenophanes says, makes gods in their own image (and so would animals, if they could). But his allegedly more rationally adequate conception of God is so peculiar – God seems to be a kind of sphere – that the issue is bound to arise of what the authority is of the reasoning that overthrows our beliefs and gets us to this point.

This question arises extremely sharply for Parmenides and Zeno of Elea, authors of some of the most notorious arguments in antiquity. Parmenides produced an abstract argument to a conclusion that nobody could accept: namely, that there is really only one object we can think of or refer to, which cannot without absurdity be said to be pluralized, qualified or divided. Thus our experience of a varied and changing plurality of objects is totally misleading. Zeno produced many arguments reducing to absurdity our everyday assumptions about plurality and change. The problem here is that the arguments are hard to fault, but the conclusions cannot be accepted. This creates a discomfort about reasoned argument: what do we do when its results conflict with our beliefs?

Responses to this differ. Some thinkers continue to produce big explanatory theories of the world, taking on board the point that their theories undermine common-sense beliefs. Anaxagoras of Clazomenae tells us that 'the Greeks are mistaken' in saying that things come into and go out of existence; in terms of his theory what emerges was there already. Similarly Empedocles of Acragas and the Atomists Leucippus and Democritus of Abdera produce theories which revise our common-sense beliefs about reality and change in accordance with their own hypotheses. None of them doubts that their reasoning has the power to do this. None of them deals adequately with the question of how we get to their theories from the beliefs we all start with – indeed Democritus recognizes a problem in that we get from our experience to the deliverances of reason, which then devalues our experience.

Other thinkers, however, including some of the sophists, fasten on the point that there is something suspicious about the way that philosophical reasoning leads by arguments that you can't fault to conclusions that you can't accept. Cleverness in argument becomes something to be feared and envied, and seen as a technique in its own right. Seen this way, there is little distinguishing philosophical reasoning from the amoral cleverness of the effective speaker in politics or the law courts.

This situation can reasonably be seen as rather a mess, and goes some way to explain why these philosophers have come to be called 'Presocratics', implying that Socrates is the crucial reference point. Whatever their individual accomplishments, they do not clearly belong within a unified tradition in which reasoning has a clear philosophical role. That begins with Socrates.

Reason and understanding

At first sight, as we have seen in Chapter 4, Socrates seems an unlikely figure to characterize the philosophical tradition. He is the perpetual amateur, who refuses to do any of the things which philosophers of his time did. Moreover, he utterly despises all these things – producing theories of the world, giving displays of oratory, winning debates – as being a pretentious waste of everybody's time. So what made him such a founding philosophical figure?

Socrates, as we have seen, argued against the views of others, showing them by their inability to withstand his arguments that they lacked understanding of what they were talking about. To have understanding of something, it emerged, you have to be able to 'give an account' of it, where this means giving reasons, and ultimately a rational account of what the subject in question is. But this will not be possible until you have rigorously asked yourself what reasons there are for the belief you hold. Thus, when you ask someone what reasons they have for what they say, you can show that they lack understanding if they have none, or have reasons that are confused or inconsistent. But, particularly if you are good at this sort of questioning (as Socrates undoubtedly was), you will realize that the same applies to you; you may have developed views, but you cannot be said to understand them, and hence have the right to put them forward authoritatively, unless you can withstand the challenges of others by giving reasons for them.

From Socrates on, reasoned argument is the lifeblood of philosophy because it is only in the give and take of argument that we achieve understanding of the positions we hold and want to put forward to others. (Understanding, as we have seen, is a kind of knowledge, and we can know only the truth; hence philosophy can also be characterized as the search for truth.) Hence the emphasis on reasoning and arguing that we find in all schools of philosophy. Now we find emerging a clear sense of *philosophical* reason and argument, distinguished from merely arguing others down and linked to the search for truth and understanding.

From the outside, then as now, all the arguing can seem aggressive and unattractive, and to those with no gift for philosophy it can seem pointless. (There is a story of a Roman bureaucrat who summoned all the Athenian philosophers and offered conflict mediation so as finally to settle all their disputes.) But from now on the importance in philosophy of reasoned argument lies in its crucial role for understanding. Figures who dismiss argument – like the Pythagoreans, who reverence their Master and want only to treasure his words – are always seen as philosophically marginal. And Epicurus' relative de-emphasis of argument led to criticism by other philosophical schools.

Philosophy as a subject

Plato has a claim to be the first philosopher to establish philosophy as a subject. He did so by taking over from Socrates two elements: argument as crucial for understanding, and positive views on a variety of matters. Plato added three other important elements. One is system, a variety of ideas seen as holding together. A second is seeing philosophy as self-consciously demarcated from other ways of thinking. And a third is the institutionalization of philosophy as a subject for study.

In the ancient world Plato was seen as a pivotal figure, the first philosopher who was concerned to systematize his ideas and thus to hold views on a wide variety of topics as holding together in a mutually supportive way. It is unclear whether it is quite fair to see Plato as the pioneer here – Democritus the Atomist also had views on a range of topics – but Plato is certainly the first to do it whose works we have. Later writers ascribed to Plato the honour of being the first to see philosophy as a system of ideas with three parts – logic, ethics and physics. This is anachronistic, but it is true that Plato held positions over most of the range that later thinkers were to cover.

Plato does not tell us how his positive systematic ideas relate to the need for understanding to be grounded by argument. But he shows us clearly enough, in writing dialogues in which he is personally never a speaker, thus detaching himself from the positions put forward, that what matters is not just having the right position, but holding it in the right way – understanding it on the basis of reasoned argument. For it is up to the reader to think about the positions put forward and test her own understanding of them. Plato, even where it is clear that he believes a position strongly, never puts it forward authoritatively. If the reader accepts it on Plato's authority, she is missing something crucial. It has to be tested and argued for before she understands it.

Plato's legacy has been a divided one. His own school, the Academy, for most of its life took philosophizing in Plato's way to be arguing against the views of contemporaries *ad hominem*, without commitment to a position of your own. It was not till after the end of the school, in the first century BC, that philosophers started to study and promote Plato's own ideas as a system. Interpretations of Plato perpetually risk overstressing one side at the expense of the other – seeing him as throwing the argument over to us, and seeing him as passionately concerned to put forward certain positions.

It is modern rather than ancient interpreters who have stressed Plato's evident desire to establish philosophy as a *distinct* way of thinking.

When he has Socrates tell us at the end of the *Republic* that there is an old quarrel between poetry (or literature more generally) and philosophy, he seems to be projecting his own view back. For one of the most striking things about Plato is the way that he is willing to use his own brilliant literary gifts to establish that philosophy is crucially about 'dialectic', sheer argument which does not rely on rhetorical or literary skill. Philosophy, he keeps insisting, is just for this reason *different* from what other people, such as orators, poets and sophists do.

Whatever the tensions this produces in Plato's own work, one of his lessons was well learned. Later philosophy develops for itself a professional style: straightforward, transparent, relying only on the force of rational argument. Unsurprisingly, this is often unattractive to ordinary readers, and we find that a gulf comes about between easier, more literary works written for the general public and 'real' philosophy, written in an uncompromisingly professional and technical way.

This gulf is also strengthened by philosophy's institutionalization. We know almost no detail about the organization of Plato's school, the Academy, though in every age philosophers have interpreted it on the model of their own university or college. But it was something new, a philosophical school, to which young men like Aristotle came to study philosophy. They probably learned Plato's ideas; they also learned how to argue. When, later in life, Aristotle set up his own philosophical school, this was seen by some as an uppity gesture, but it established the pattern whereby an original philosopher would set up his own school, finding pupils and disciples who would learn, further and spread his ideas. Hence Plato's philosophy and Aristotle's philosophy came to have a history in their own schools; they became objects of study to other philosophers.

Once we get schools of philosophy – the Stoic and Epicurean schools getting established on similar principles – we can see the activity of ancient philosophers as astonishingly like the activity of modern philosophers. Although Plato, who was rich, refused to take fees for teaching, payment by pupils soon became a necessary feature of the system. Young men (and occasionally young women) would join a philosophical school as part of their education. (Or they might have a trained philosopher as a tutor at home.) They were educated to understand and appreciate important philosophical ideas, many of which were already part of their cultural heritage. In the schools, they were also trained in argument, acquiring abilities which had more practical application when they left, in politics and law, for example. Those most gifted at philosophy, and committed to it, would stay and become part of the school's permanent philosophical community. This does not sound so unlike the picture of philosophy teaching in universities today. (Or rather, in the less rigid university system that existed before degrees and grades came to be important as credentials.) This idea of philosophy as a kind of university education continued on until late in the ancient world, throughout vast political and cultural changes.

The similarity extends to many of the specific ways in which philosophy was carried on. We find philosophers writing treatises and essays, and also books of arguments against other philosophers' treatises and essays. We find commentaries on texts of past philosophers, especially Plato and Aristotle. We find controversies within a school, for example as to which of two contemporaries has got Epicurus right. We also find extensive arguments against other contemporary schools. In their style and purpose many of these works are quite like modern philosophy journal articles and books. Indeed, modern philosophy students can find it easier to relate to works of this kind, the products of philosophical professionalism, than to Plato's dialogues, which are in form unlike any modern kind of philosophical writing.

Philosophy after Plato is, then, the history of philosophical schools (with two exceptions, to which we shall return). There is an interesting shadow side to it – a running complaint till the end of antiquity about

Ancient Philosophy

bogus philosophers, who use philosophy's prestige to further their private agenda, whether money or reputation. The bogus philosopher, high-minded in class and money-grubbing outside it, is a stock figure of ridicule. This brings home the fact that in the ancient world philosophy was taken to offer people not only intellectual challenge but also practical help in living a better life and finding answers to the search for the meaning of life. Philosophers were expected not only to convey intellectual skills but also to provide in their own persons examples of the search for living well. Nowadays we are more likely to seek the latter in religion, or in less intellectual pursuits. Ancient philosophers did not offer just one subject among many, but a subject that was uniquely close to the hearts of their audience.

A diverse range of schools

Although Aristotle was Plato's pupil, in some ways his is the least representative of the schools which formed after the Academy. This is because of Aristotle's own huge range of interests. He studied, furthered or invented a wide range of subjects, from literary theory to logic, from economics to biology. The works he left behind are vast, some of them theoretical treatises and others more like records of research. In this respect Aristotle's school differs from the philosophical schools that come after him, which had narrower interests.

The Stoics' school began, as the earlier ones had, in a public place; Epicurus was unusual in holding his school in a private residence, the Garden. And Epicurus was unusual also in requiring his views to be held deferentially and memorized. But before very long the Epicurean school and its offshoots in other places were doing very similar things to the Stoics and other schools – arguing and counter-arguing, commenting on founding texts, generally continuing the philosophical activity of the founders. Every generation of students needs to learn afresh and understand philosophical positions for themselves, and hence even philosophical schools dedicated to teaching the thought of the founders will develop philosophically in the give and take of philosophical interpretation. Moreover, with changing political and social circumstances new issues had to be dealt with and new challenges met. When the Romans became rulers of the Mediterranean, for example, Greek intellectuals started educating unintellectual Romans.

From the first century BC we find that the continuing debates between the schools give rise to some schools which are hybrids, or 'eclectic' – combining positions from different schools to form a new stance. One who was influential in his day was Antiochus, who thought that the core

8. Philosophers discussing and arguing together

views of Plato, Aristotle and the Stoics on a number of issues were compatible, and that the differences had been overplayed. Histories of philosophy tend to rank these schools lower in interest than those founded by more original thinkers. But we can sympathize with their position. Once philosophy has formed a teaching tradition, it can well seem foolish to seek originality at all costs, and sounder to argue from and build on what are already going positions. This is what most philosophers do today, so we should pause before turning up our noses at it.

In the late Roman republic and early Empire, ancient philosophy arguably had a heyday. There were no more great original thinkers, but a variety of philosophical schools flourished and interacted. A serious student would have widespread opportunities to learn and think about the ideas of a variety of philosophical schools spread throughout the Roman Empire. (By this time Athens had lost its previous dominance as a centre of philosophy, which it had held from Plato to the first century BC, and cities like Alexandria and Rome itself were as important intellectually.) Philosophy was familiar and accessible to educated people throughout the Empire. It has seldom been the case that so rich and varied an intellectual tradition has been so culturally widespread and so important to many people. Until the end of antiquity the only significant new school was a third century AD reformulation of an old one – Plotinus' rethinking of Plato's ideas in a new and original synthesis, giving rise to the school we call Neoplatonism, one which flourished in later centuries.

In the mix were two philosophical movements mentioned earlier, which were anti-schools rather than schools.

The first of these movements is Pyrrhonian scepticism, which, as we saw in Chapter 4, was a breakaway movement from the scepticism of Plato's Academy. Pyrrhonism is perfectly viable as a methodology, and as such can be systematized, rather as we find it in our main source, Sextus

Empiricus. But in its own terms it is self-defeating for a Pyrrhonist to set up as an authority on anything, even the nature of Pyrrhonism. For this would convict him of firm enough commitment to some beliefs to threaten sceptical tranquillity. Hence Pyrrhonism could never coherently be an institutionalized school. This is one reason why we know so little about its spread and influence.

The second 'anti-school' movement is the Cynics, deriving from the fourth-century figure Diogenes of Sinope, who set a model which was followed rather than setting up any formal institution. Cynics took their name from dogs (the ancient symbol of shamelessness), went in for street preaching and lived in ways which deliberately flouted social norms, the aim being to 'return to nature' by rejecting social convention. Some Cynics did teach informally, but as a philosophy it remained a way of life, attracting moralizing drop-outs. It could never be a philosophical school, since Cynics rejected reasoned argument, taking it that there is really nothing difficult to understand and that the answers to life's problems are simple.

The final break

The end of ancient philosophy as a living tradition is hard to date, especially since the end of antiquity – the culture of Greece and Rome – is also not something to which a neat date can be given. When the Roman Empire split, the Eastern, Byzantine empire retained political and cultural unity, and philosophy remained there as an academic study, though in partial and restricted form. In the Western part all such unity crumbled, and philosophical texts were (some of them) preserved in monasteries by people who were no longer part of the tradition they contained. Even knowledge of Greek, the language of the major texts, was lost. When philosophy developed again, some of the tradition, mainly Aristotle and some Plato, became part of it, but within a different, theological framework. Not until the Renaissance did it become possible to study the ancient texts independently, and study of

Aristotle still has to contend with the after-effects of his medieval transformation.

There is therefore something to be said for dating the end of ancient philosophy, as a living tradition, in AD 529, the year in which the Christian Emperor Justinian closed the schools of pagan philosophy in Athens. Like many famous historical moments, this one crumbles somewhat under historical investigation. Athens had long ceased to be the major philosophical centre; it is not clear that any philosophical schools were functioning there other than the Platonists; Justinian did not actually close the schools, but at most seems to have forbidden pagans to teach, and the decree does not seem to have been effective. Pagan philosophy was in trouble before 529, and trickled on to some extent afterwards.

9. On a Christian tomb, a philosopher sits next to a praying figure

Yet there is a rightness to the idea that it was intolerance by a Christian Emperor that marked the tradition's end. Jews and Christians in the ancient world had always faced a choice between rejecting philosophy entirely in favour of faith and loyalty to scripture, and trying to incorporate at least some philosophy into their own traditions. They did this by claiming that philosophy was a development in distorted form of some of the deep truths in Judaism and Christianity. Such an approach, however, is not only selective but curtails drastically the space for reason and argument, always so central to the activity of ancient philosophers. Jewish and Christian writers in the ancient world have by and large served as transmitters to us of (parts of) the philosophical tradition, rather than as participants in it. With Christianity a single intellectual view of the world was imposed, and philosophy was mostly unable to continue its task of questioning and reasoning about our beliefs.

Ancient philosophy and philosophy today

Since its recovery, ancient philosophy has played a mostly respected and occasionally influential role in the development of philosophy in Western European countries, which have seen themselves as the inheritors of the culture of the ancient Greek and Roman world, and also in philosophy in countries culturally influenced by Western Europe, such as North America and Australia. Different parts of the hugely varied ancient tradition have been found compelling at different times. The Stoics were influential in the eighteenth century, relegated to specialist studies in the nineteenth; exactly the opposite happened to Plato. At times the idea of Great Thinkers has led to a view of 'the canon' as a parade of Great Thoughts, to the neglect of their argumentative context. The tradition has been capacious enough to give rise to an variety of differing engagements – all, for the last three centuries at least, appreciating the importance to it of reasoned argument for philosophical understanding.

There has, however, been one unfortunate result of this stress on reason and argument. It has sometimes given rise, in the later ancient world and also in the twentieth century, to a simplifying tendency to see other philosophical traditions, particularly 'Eastern' ones, as radically different and 'other', characterized by lessened emphasis on argument and a greater stress on mysticism and a search for wisdom by non-rational means. This has sometimes led to the view that they are more primitive than the 'Western' tradition, because it honours reason. But it has also led, by reaction, to the view that they are more profound than the 'Western' tradition, which prizes what gets seen as superficial squabbling. In the late twentieth century especially, sweeping attacks have been made on reason and its place in the 'Western' tradition, and ancient philosophy has often been the subject of (usually ill-informed) attacks.

Both tendencies have been unfortunate; they lead to crude contrasts which are unhelpful and in large part untrue. This holds particularly with respect to the philosophy of India. Ancient India produced a large and wide philosophical tradition, encompassing materialism, scepticism and empiricism as well as schools tending to mysticism and forms of idealism – a tradition which is comparable to ancient Greek and Roman philosophy in extent and variety. Yet both Westerners and many Indians have (unless they are specialists) emphasized only those schools that form a contrast to Western philosophy. Students often think that 'Eastern' philosophy, including Indian, will be all similar and nothing like the 'Western' tradition. We have yet to reach a completely post-colonial view, which can get beyond the false contrast of 'Western rationalism' and 'Eastern mysticism' and recognizes the strong affinities between some of the Indian traditions and ancient Greek and Roman traditions more familiar in the West. (It has been suggested, for example, that there are affinities between Pyrrhonian scepticism and the Madhyamika school of North Indian Buddhism, whose founding figure is Nagarjuna, who was perhaps contemporary with Sextus Empiricus. In view of the story that Pyrrho earlier visited North India with Alexander's army, there is even the possibility of historical influences on both sides, particularly given the continued Greek presence in Northern India.)

I shall close with a view of ancient philosophy by an intellectual insider with an outsider's perspective – Lucian of Samosata, a second century AD satirical author. In his essay *The Runaways* he has Philosophy remind her father, the chief god Zeus, of the reason he sent her down to earth in the first place, namely so that humans, hitherto ignorantly and violently mismanaging their lives, would do better. First, she continues, she went to India, to the Brahmans, then to Ethiopia, Egypt and Babylon, and then to Thrace, the wild north. Finally she went to the Greeks, which she had thought would be the easy part, given their intellectual reputation. But it turned out to be harder than she expected. After a promising start, the Sophists mixed philosophy up with – well, sophistry. And then the Athenians executed Socrates! Philosophy goes on to complain about the less than wonderful time she went on to have in Greece. Most people respect her, she says, though without much understanding her, and there are genuine philosophers who love and strive for truth, and this makes it all worth while. But there are also bogus philosophers who aim only at money and status, and bring her into discredit, and they drive her crazy. She needs a bit of divine help to improve the situation.

In the ancient Greco-Roman world philosophy, for better and worse, became a subject, with its own practices, texts and institutions. It was a more urgent matter to its practitioners and its audience than it is for us now. Philosophy was seen as a natural extension of an ordinary good education, given the importance of living well, and the importance of philosophy for doing that. For us there is more of a tension than there was for the ancients between the idea that philosophy enables us to understand ourselves and the world, and the idea that it is a rigorous and intellectually demanding matter. The important role in life played by philosophy in the ancient world has been taken over by a variety of other interests and pursuits. But philosophy still matters, and in many

Ancient Philosophy

116

ways we can still relate our concerns to those of the ancients, and find that our study of them leads naturally to direct philosophical engagement. We still have Philosophy's problem and, lacking divine help, we still have to do the work, search for the truth, and expose the bogus for ourselves.

Timeline

600 BC	550 BC	500 BC	450 BC	400 BC	350 BC	300 BC	250 BC	200 BC
	Thales	Parmenides		Diogenes of Sinope			Chrysippus	Arcesilaus
	Xenophanes	Zeno of Elea		(The Cynic)			Archimedes	Carneades
	Anaximander	Heraclitus		Aristotle				
	Anaximenes	Empedocles			Theophrastus			
	Pythagoras	Anaxagoras			Pyrrho			
			Socrates		Epicurus			
			Aristippus			Zeno of Citium		
			Democritus					
			Antisthenes					
			Plato					

150 BC	100 BC	50 BC	AD 1	AD 50	AD 100	AD 150	AD 200	AD 250
	Antiochus		Seneca	Epictetus		Sextus Empiricus	Plotinus	
	Cicero							

AD 300	AD 350	AD 400	AD 450	AD 500	AD 550
	Augustine				

Further Reading

The fragments of the Presocratics can be read in Jonathan Barnes's *Early Greek Philosophy* (London, 1987) and in Richard McKirahan's *Philosophy Before Socrates* (Indianapolis, 1994). The McKirahan collection contains commentary, and an excellent philosophical introduction is Jonathan Barnes's *The Presocratic Philosophers* (London, 1979).

Plato's dialogues can be best read in *Plato: Complete Works*, ed. J. Cooper and D. Hutchinson (Indianapolis, 1998). There are also good translations of single dialogues, with commentaries and introductions, published by Oxford (in the World's Classics series), Penguin, and Hackett. A good introduction is *The Cambridge Companion to Plato*, ed. Richard Kraut (Cambridge, 1992).

The standard translation of Aristotle is the revised Oxford translation, to be found in *The Complete Works of Aristotle*, ed. Jonathan Barnes (Princeton, 1984). *Aristotle: Selections*, ed. T. Irwin and G. Fine (Indianapolis, 1995) is a good introductory selection. A good introduction is *The Cambridge Companion to Aristotle*, ed. Jonathan Barnes (Cambridge, 1995).

Stoics, Epicureans and Sceptics can be read in B. Inwood and L. Gerson, *Hellenistic Philosophy* (Indianapolis, 1997), and also in A. A. Long and D. Sedley, *The Hellenistic Philosophers* (Cambridge, 1987). There is unfortunately no good English collection of the fragments of the

Cyrenaics. For Pyrrhonism see *Sextus Empiricus: Outlines of Scepticism*, trans. Julia Annas and Jonathan Barnes (Cambridge, 1994), and also *The Modes of Scepticism* (Cambridge, 1985) by the same authors. A good introduction is R. Sharples, *Stoics, Epicureans, Sceptics* (London, 1996). For Middle Platonism see John Dillon, *The Middle Platonists* (Ithaca, 1997), and for Neoplatonism see R. T. Wallis, *Neoplatonism* (London, 1972).

Ancient philosophy is so varied that there is no good detailed history of the entire tradition by a single author. A very brief introduction is T. Irwin, *Classical Thought* (Oxford, 1989). Also good is C. Gill, *Greek Thought* (Oxford, 1995). W. K. C. Guthrie's six-volume *History of Greek Philosophy* (Cambridge, 1962–1981), ends at Aristotle and is uncritical, but is a good guide to sources. Histories of ancient philosophy have for some time taken the form of studies of particular philosophies or issues, rather than a single narrative of the whole tradition. Many can be found in the bibliographies of the works mentioned below.

A introductory reader, with texts arranged round issues rather than chronologically, is Julia Annas, *Ancient Voices of Philosophy* (Oxford, 2000). A more comprehensive reader for advanced students, also arranged topically, is Terence Irwin, *Classical Philosophy* (Oxford, 1999).

Chapters on philosophy at various periods can be found in the *Oxford History of the Classical World* (Oxford, 1986). Excellent reference works are the *Oxford Classical Dictionary,* 3rd edition (Oxford, 1996), and *The Encyclopaedia of Classical Philosophy,* ed. Don Zeyl (Westport, 1996).

The forthcoming multi-author *Cambridge History of Hellenistic Philosophy* and *Cambridge History of Greek and Roman Political Thought* are good guides to the areas they cover.

An extremely useful series is the *Cambridge Companions to Ancient Thought,* edited by Stephen Everson. These are *Epistemology* (1990), *Psychology* (1991), *Language* (1994) and *Ethics* (1998).

Notes

The Notes mention only authors and topics not covered in the Further Reading.

Chapter 1

Euripides' play is available in many modern translations. The Epictetus passages are *Discourses* I 28 and II 17; many modern translations are available. Plato's account of the divided soul can be found in Books 4 and 9 of the *Republic*, and in *Phaedrus*, especially 244–257; also in parts of *Timaeus*. Galen's comments are from his *On the doctrines of Hippocrates and Plato* III 3; there is a translation in the *Corpus Medicorum Graecorum*, the collected texts and translations of Greek medical writers. For further explorations of this theme in ancient philosophy see A. Price, *Mental Conflict* (Oxford, 1995), and C. Gill, *Personality in Greek Epic, Tragedy and Philosophy* (Oxford, 1996), especially Chapters 3 and 4.

Chapter 2

The case for seeing the *Republic* as primarily an ethical work, as in the ancient tradition, is developed in Chapter 4 of Julia Annas, *Platonic Ethics Old and New* (Ithaca, 1999).

There has been extensive work on the impact of ancient Greek culture on the Victorians, but there is little good on ancient philosophy. Of the available books, the best is Frank Turner, *The Greek Heritage in Victorian*

Britain (New Haven, 1981); see also his article, 'Why the Greeks and not the Romans in Victorian Britain?' in G. W. Clarke (ed.), *Rediscovering Hellenism: the Hellenic inheritance and the English imagination* (Cambridge, 1989).

On the role of the Utilitarians see Kyriakos Demetriou, 'The Development of Platonic Studies in Britain and the Role of the Utilitarians', *Utilitas* 8 (1996). Two excellent articles are John Glucker, 'Plato in England: the Nineteenth Century and After', in H. Funke (ed.), *Utopie und Tradition: Platons Lehre vom Staat in der Moderne* (Würzburg, 1987) and 'The Two Platos of Victorian Britain', in K. Algra *et al.* (eds.), *Polyhistor* (Leiden, 1996).

I have considered England; for the early American tradition see Carl J. Richard, *The Founders and the Classics* (Cambridge MA, 1994). The European tradition differs between countries and is highly complex: see the papers in Ada Neschke-Hentschke (ed.), *Images de Platon et Lectures de ses Oeuvres: les interprétations de Platon à travers les siècles* (Louvain-Paris, 1997.

Grote's *Plato* and John Stuart Mill's long review of it are still richly rewarding; see Mill's *Collected Works*, vol XI (Toronto, 1978).

The quotations from Popper are from *The Open Society and its Enemies*, vol 1 (London, 1945). John Wild's book was published in Chicago in 1953. Whitehead's very famous remark is from *Process and Reality* (Cambridge, 1929), Part 2, chapter 1, section 1. The *History of the University of Oxford* is edited by T. Aston, and the quotation is from p. 529 of vol. 5, *The Eighteenth Century* (Oxford, 1986).

Chapter 3

Xenophon's story comes from his *Memorabilia (Reminiscences of Socrates)*, Book II, 1. Evidence for the sophists' ideas can be found in R. McKirahan's *Philosophy before Socrates* (Indianapolis, 1994). Ancient eudaimonist theories are set out and discussed in Julia Annas, *The Morality of Happiness* (Oxford, 1993). Aristotle's major theoretical discussion of happiness is in Book 1 of the *Nicomachean Ethics*. The views of Epicurus and the Stoics on happiness are best studied in books 1–4 of Cicero's *On Moral Ends* (*De Finibus*); see the English translation by Raphael Woolf (Cambridge, 2001).

Chapter 4

On Socrates see Christopher Taylor's *Socrates* (Oxford. 1998), an excellent short introduction. Socrates' own account of the oracle is in the *Apology*. Socrates served as the symbolic figure of the ideal philosopher for most ancient schools; the Epicureans are the main exception; for them the ideal philosopher should be as serious and unironic as Epicurus. Plato's most elaborate account of knowledge is in the central books of the *Republic*; his attacks on relativism, and indications of his concern with empirical knowledge, are in the *Theaetetus*. Aristotle's discussion of the structure of a science is in the difficult *Posterior Analytics*; see also the opening chapters of Books 1 and 2 of the *Metaphysics* for his account of the development of knowledge, and *Parts of Animals*, Book 1, chapter 5, for a defence of studying widely differing kinds of subject-matter. An indispensable introduction to the wide range of ancient theories of knowledge is S. Everson (ed.), *Epistemology* (Cambridge, 1990).

Chapter 5

For Aristotle's logic see Robin Smith's translation of the *Prior Analytics* (Indianapolis, 1989) and his chapter in the *Cambridge Companion to Aristotle*, ed. J. Barnes (Cambridge, 1995). There is unfortunately no good English translation of the sources for Stoic logic; see the relevant sections of Inwood and Gerson, and of Long and Sedley. The sources are collected in Karlheinz Hülser, *Die Fragmente der Dialektiker der Stoiker*, 4 vols (Stuttgart, 1987).

On Hellenistic science see G. Lloyd, *Greek Science after Aristotle* (London,

1973). For clear introductions to Aristotle's metaphysics and philosophy of science see the chapters in the *Cambridge Companion to Aristotle*. There is little sustained philosophical discussion of Stoic and Epicurean metaphysics; there is, by contrast, a huge literature on Plato's 'theory of Forms': see the *Cambridge Companion to Plato*.

Chapter 6

The Further Reading gives suggestions for following up the history of ancient philosophy. The quotation from Martin West is from 'Early Greek Philosophy', in *The Oxford History of Greece and the Hellenistic World*, (Oxford, 1986). The comment that Plato is just Moses in Greek is fragment 8 of Numenius, a second-century Platonist who tended to see all Great Ideas in different cultures as being the same. Eusebius, in X 1 and XI 1 of his *Preparation for the Gospel*, claims more strongly that Greek philosophy steals all its ideas from the Jewish scriptures. The contrasting quotations about the nature of the beginnings of Greek philosophy are from John Burnet, *Early Greek Philosophy* (London, 1892) pp. v, 13, 28, and from Francis Cornford, *Principium Sapientiae: a study of the origins of Greek philosophical thought* (Cambridge, 1952) pp. 154–155.

Index

Index

133

Expand your collection of
VERY SHORT INTRODUCTIONS

Visit the
VERY SHORT INTRODUCTIONS
Web site

www.oup.co.uk/vsi

➤ **Information** about all published titles

➤ News of **forthcoming books**

➤ **Extracts** from the books, including titles not yet published

➤ **Reviews** and views

➤ **Links** to other **web sites** and main OUP web page

➤ Information about **VSIs in translation**

➤ **Contact** the editors

➤ **Order** other **VSIs** on-line

CLASSICS
A Very Short Introduction

Mary Beard and John Henderson

This Very Short Introduction to Classics links a
haunting temple on a lonely mountainside to the glory
of ancient Greece and the grandeur of Rome, and to
Classics within modern culture – from Jefferson and
Byron to Asterix and Ben-Hur.

'The authors show us that Classics is a "modern" and
sexy subject. They succeed brilliantly in this regard …
nobody could fail to be informed and entertained – and
the accent of the book is provocative and stimulating.'

John Godwin, *Times Literary Supplement*

'Statues and slavery, temples and tragedies, museum,
marbles, and mythology – this provocative guide to the
Classics demysties its varied subject-matter while
seducing the reader with the obvious enthusiasm and
pleasure which mark its writing.'

Edith Hall

www.oup.co.uk/vsi/classics